DAVII

T H E
N E W
O L D

How the Boomers
Are Changing
Everything ... Again

Published by ECW Press
2120 Queen Street East, Suite 200
Toronto, Ontario, Canada M4E 1E2
416.694.3348 / info@ecwpress.com

LIBRARY AND ARCHIVES CANADA CATALOGUING IN PUBLICATION

Cravit, David
The new old : how the boomers are changing everything . . . again / David Cravit.

ISBN 978-1-55022-843-4

1. Baby boom generation. 2. Middle-aged persons—Social conditions. 3. Middle age—
Social aspects. 4. Aging. I. Title.

HQ1061.C72 2008   305.244   C2008-902385-4

Cover Design: Paul Hodgson
Cover photo: I. Rozenbaum & F. Cirou / Jupiter Images
Interior photos: Diane Keaton - David Gabber/PR Photos;
Mick Jagger - Solarpix/PR Photos; snake (page 13) - drawing by Rachel Cravit;
all other interior images courtesy of the author.
Text Design: Michael Betteridge
Typesetting: Gail Nina
Printing: Thomson-Shore

The publication of *The New Old* has been generously supported by the Government of
Ontario through Ontario Book Publishing Tax Credit, by the OMDC Book Fund, an
initiative of the Ontario Media Development Corporation, and by the Government of
Canada through the Book Publishing Industry Development Program (BPIDP).

Canadä

PRINTED AND BOUND IN THE UNITED STATES

ECW PRESS
ecwpress.com

In memory of my mother

Ruth Lappin Cravit
1919–1962

who would have been a Zoomer

ACKNOWLEDGMENTS

I have been fortunate to work with a company that has given me a ringside seat to the phenomenon of BoomerAging and the transformation of "seniors" into "Zoomers." To my colleagues at ZoomerMedia — and in particular Moses Znaimer, who has taught, encouraged and challenged me all at the same time — my sincerest thanks.

I am also grateful for the help and encouragement I received in connection with the development and marketing of this book, and I particularly want to acknowledge Syd Kessler, David Sersta and Howard Szigeti.

I want to thank my agent, Don Bastian, for identifying the potential in this project at a very early stage, and for getting it into presentable shape, and my publisher, Jack David, for his unfailing patience and good counsel. I appreciate the hard work of Jack's team at ECW Press, and want to acknowledge Rachel Ironstone and Crissy Boylan.

Above all, I owe a tremendous debt of gratitude to my family. My wife Cynthia, in her position as ZoomerMedia's online editor, has been the source of a huge array of fascinating stories, factoids, web links and other valuable insights into all the wild and wonderful things going on out there. She is also my soul mate, best friend, toughest critic and unfailing cheerleader when I need it the most. My children — Tammy, Joanna, Rachel, Nathaniel and Nicholas — could always be counted on for encouragement and support (and in Rachel's case, artwork, too!). No Zoomer could be luckier!

TABLE OF CONTENTS

PART ONE: HOW DID WE GET HERE?

CHAPTER 1 **The big picture**

In 1952, the first year of Queen Elizabeth's reign, she sent a congratulatory letter to 255 people on the occasion of their 100th birthday. She also sent congratulatory letters to 2,745 couples celebrating their diamond (60th) wedding anniversary.

In 2005, the Queen congratulated 6,914 people for hitting the century mark, and a further 24,304 couples celebrating 60 years of marriage. She also sent congratulations to 576 people for reaching the age of 105 — more than double the number of people who had reached a measly 100 when the Queen first got going.

Here's a graph of the Queen's trendline:

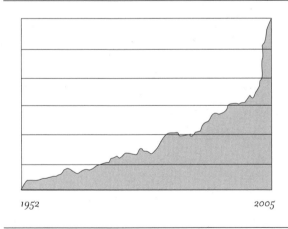

Fig. 1 — Number of congratulatory messages sent to very old people by Queen Elizabeth, 1952–2005

1952   *2005*

I offer this as my version of the proof that the population is aging.

But you already know that, don't you?

You can't pick up a newspaper or business magazine these days without reading about it. From marketers to think tank gurus, from politicians to statisticians, from journalists to social workers, everyone has "suddenly" discovered Boomers and seniors.

People are living longer, obviously, so "older people" represent an ever-increasing percentage of the population. This is expected to put huge burdens on existing pension programs, health care systems and other social agencies. Most of what's being written about the aging of the population focuses on *numbers* — the number of people hitting retirement age, the dollar extent to which they're underfunded (and are they ever), the costs of future medical care, pensions and other entitlement programs, percentages up and down, a glut of statistics.

True, there are plenty of articles about Baby Boomers and seniors as a market (still largely ignored by the media and advertising industries), and their wealth and purchasing power. And there have been a few books about the impact of Boomers on society — individualism, diversity, tolerance, fanatic work ethic, shameless self-absorption.

But for the most part, the aging of the population is seen largely as a matter of arithmetic — more old people, and therefore more problems associated with being old.

Do we really need another book on that theme?

If not, what's my angle? Why should you pay attention?

I believe the big story isn't *how many* "older people" there are. It's *who* they are.

An astonishing process is underway today. It's just starting to take shape, and its influence will be felt for centuries — maybe forever. The process is being carried out by the demographic segment that has been poked, prodded, analyzed, loved and hated more than any other group in history — the Baby Boomers.

What the Boomers are doing is, quite simply, destroying our entire concept of aging. The Boomers are, in effect, *de-aging*. And, since the Boomers gleefully "own" whatever it is they're doing at any point in time, we can readily make their name a part of the label — I call it BoomerAging.

And the differences between "aging" and "BoomerAging" aren't subtle, either. As we'll see, by the time the Boomers get done, *all* of our age-related ideas and norms will be replaced:

- The definition of "aging" and "old age"
- The "expected" patterns of behavior that have always been attached to aging
- The concept of retirement and employment
- The nature, structure and timeline of education
- Product development, marketing and communication
- The health care system
- Sex
- Money
- And just about *all* government policy (hint: they're already missing the boat)

These changes will be *permanent*, too. As a result of what the Boomers are pioneering, being "old" will never mean the same thing again. Thus, the title of this book: the *new* old.

In the world of The New Old . . .

- The idea of being "older" will start much later than ever before.
- It will be characterized by attitudes, behaviors and patterns of spending that we have never seen before.
- It will shatter the assumptions, structures and conducts of business of virtually every industry and every area of government responsibility.

It's not exactly a modest assertion that I'm making.

So before we get started, let's clean up a few details so as to lay the proper groundwork.

What makes me such an expert?

In the first place, I'm a Baby Boomer myself. I'm living through all of the phenomena I'm about to lay out for you.

As Executive Vice-President of ZoomerMedia, I'm in charge of sales and marketing for Canada's largest media company specializing in . . .

Ah.

There's the first wrinkle.

When I first wrote this manuscript I wrote ". . . specializing in Baby Boomers and seniors."

That phrase was perfectly OK with my publisher, and it duly made it into the first version of the typeset layout.

Then the President of my company, Moses Znaimer — easily Canada's foremost media genius — popularized the term "Zoomers" to describe this audience. He started with the idea of "Boomers with Zip" but it quickly expanded to include the entire population of Baby Boomers and everyone older. Within barely a month, the term had spread like wildfire and was eagerly being embraced by the media as well as by virtually everyone who had previously been described as "senior," "elderly," "mature," "Golden Age" and other equally depressing terms. In the next chapter, I'll go into a lot more detail about what Moses did and how and why it's taking off so dramatically. For now, let me just note that we specialize in this market — it's our only business. (They were all babies when, in 1948, Gerber adopted as its ad slogan, "Babies are our business . . . our only business" — but of course you'd have to be a Zoomer to remember that!) Our multiple web sites and electronic newsletters generate over a million page views a month. You can find out all about us, and link to our various media properties, at www.zoomermedia.ca.

We also handle communications and marketing for CARP, Canada's largest association for . . .

Ah. Again a need to define this audience.

CARP originally stood for Canada's Association for Retired Persons. Then they changed it to Canada's Association for the 50-Plus. Then along came Moses Znaimer and the magic term, Zoomers. So CARP is now Canada's Association for Zoomers.

We own and publish CARP's magazine — rebranded as *ZOOMER* magazine in October 2008 — and CARP's website and electronic newsletter. We also manage CARP's member benefits program.

Since CARP is the Canadian affiliate of the AARP Global Network, we also work closely with AARP in the USA, and dialogue frequently with 50-plus and "seniors" associations around the world.

So I deal exclusively with this market — and I bring more than 30 years of prior experience in advertising and marketing, in both Canada and the

USA, to the topic.

Because such a big part of our business is online, we can track exactly what our audience is reading. We know what topics interest them, and what topics don't. We know exactly how much time they spend exploring which subjects, where they land and where they click to go next, what questions they're asking, what information they're searching for. We also conduct extensive research, both online and offline, giving us valuable additional insights into what makes this age group tick.

You may not agree with everything I have to say.

But I will back it up. And at the very minimum, I'll provide you with some fresh and (hopefully) provocative challenges to the assumptions you and your organization are currently working with.

If you think you've figured out "the aging of the population," I intend to show you that it's a much bigger issue, with much more far-reaching implications, than you may have imagined. Whether you work in the private sector or public sector, whether your goal is to make money or provide social services, what the Boomers are doing to the process of aging today will call for a profound re-thinking of *everything* you're doing.

Who are we talking about, exactly?

Everybody has a sense of what we mean when we say "Boomers" or "Baby Boomers" — people born after World War II, when there was a dramatic increase in the birth rate in Canada, the USA and the UK.

But there's no uniform agreement, among demographers, as to the precise start and end dates of the phenomenon. How big a drop in the birth rate had to occur before you could officially declare that the "boom" was over? What if there was a rebound? In the UK, for example, there was a huge population surge in 1946, 1947 and 1948, followed by a drop, then another surge in the early 1960s. Was the second surge part of the "original" Baby Boom or a whole new group?

To see how complicated it can get, take a look at this table. It's far from being an exhaustive summary of the state of play; it's simply meant to serve as a quick overview of how much variation is possible if you want to slice and

Country	Authority	Baby Boom dates	Comments
USA	*Boomer Nation*, by Steve Gillen	1946–1964	Creates two groups: Boomers (born 1945–1957) and Shadow Boomers (born 1958–1964)
USA	*Marketing to Leading-Edge Baby Boomers* by Brent Green	1946–1965	Again, creates two groups: Leading-Edge Boomers (born 1946–1955) and Trailing-Edge Boomers (born 1956–1965)
USA	*Generations* by William Strauss and Neil Howe	1943–1960	Include those conceived by soldiers home on leave
Canada	David Foot	1947–1966	Best-selling author of *Boom, Bust, Echo*
Canada	Pierre Fortin	1945–1960	Professor of Economics, University of Montreal

Table 1 — A sample of definitions of when the "Baby Boom" occurred.

dice the statistics finely enough.

And we could keep on going . . .

We have to settle somewhere. So in this book, we'll define Boomers two ways:

(a) By dates

We'll use "post-World War II until the early 1960s" as an adequate definition.

(b) By landmark events and icons

I find this a more interesting (if statistically less rigorous) approach, because it allows for "spillover" influence on people slightly older or slightly younger, but who nevertheless were defined by the Baby Boomer experience and mindset. Using this approach, if you were in your early 20s by the time the following had happened, you're a Boomer:

• Assassination of JFK, RFK and Martin Luther King
• Walk on the moon

- Vietnam War
- Woodstock
- Rock 'n' roll
- The Beatles
- Watergate
- "Make love, not war"
- Pierre Elliott Trudeau
- "Tune in, turn on, drop out"
- "I'd like to buy the world a Coke"

Or we can come at it from the direction of Boomer personalities. If you're roughly the same age as any of the following, you're a Boomer:

- Bill Clinton
- George Bush
- Tony Blair
- Osama bin Laden
- Vladimir Putin
- Prince Charles
- Stephen Harper
- Richard Branson
- Elton John
- David Bowie
- John Travolta
- Stephen Spielberg
- Bill Gates
- Emmy Lou Harris
- Madonna
- Oprah Winfrey
- Françoise Hardy
- Jerry Seinfeld
- Bruce Springsteen
- Ozzy Osbourne
- Tom Hanks

I think you get the idea.

Under either (a) or (b), we wind up with approximately . . .

· 8 million Canadians
· 75 million Americans
· 17 million Brits

That's 100 million people, give or take, or about 25% of the total pop-ulation of the three countries combined.

Culturally or attitudinally, I think we could add those born during World War II — they are certainly being influenced in their own attitudes and behavior by what the Boomers are doing. So this might push us to about a third of the population of the USA, Canada and the UK.

But surely they don't all behave the same way?

True — and a very fair point.

But this is a book about the trendsetters. The leading edge. The people who are breaking the mold.

I can certainly demonstrate that, statistically, there are more than enough of them to be wielding the huge influence I'm assigning to them. You'll be satisfied that we're not talking about a handful of oddballs or zealots here. That said, this is *not* an attempt to drown you in statistics in order to "prove" a set of numbers.

Are there millions of Baby Boomers who are *not* breaking new ground, and are instead behaving like "old people" of previous generations behaved? Absolutely.

Are there millions of Boomers who are too poor, or too sick, or other-wise unable to participate fully in this re-definition aging? No question about it.

But my case doesn't depend on piling up numbers to arrive at some magic moment of "Aha!" where I show that 51% (or any other arbitrary per-centage) of Boomers fit my thesis. There simply have to be enough of them to be an irresistible force for change — to have certain attitudes and expec-tations, to live a certain way, so as to open up entirely new possibilities of what it means to age and to impose those new possibilities on the process of aging today, as well as for all future generations. And I'll offer more than enough evidence to convince you of that.

So here we go with the Baby Boomers again. Isn't it just a matter of their self-absorption, their massive narcissism, making them *pretend* they're not really getting old? Aren't you building this up to way more than it really is?
Another perfectly fair question — and one that we'll circle back to, more than once, in the course of this book.

The Boomers were the original "Me" generation. They were raised by parents who had suffered through the Great Depression and World War II, and who, for the most part, didn't want to see their darlings undergo the same hardships. They were also lucky enough to be born into decades of peace and prosperity (though with the underlying nervousness of the Cold War and the possibilities of a nuclear holocaust at any time). They were pampered, no question about it, and conditioned to believe there was nothing they couldn't have.

Not surprisingly, this has provoked some strong hostility. Here's Paul Begala, who worked as a consultant to the ultimate Baby Boomer, President Bill Clinton:

> I've spent my whole life swimming behind that garbage barge of a generation. They ruined everything they've passed through and left me in their wake. . . . At the risk of feeding their narcissism, I believe it's time someone stated the simple truth: The Baby Boomers are the most self-centered, self-seeking, self-interested, self-absorbed, self-indulgent, self-aggrandizing generation in American history. I hate the Boomers.

So, yes, it would be easy to argue that I'm going way too far when I claim the Boomers are doing anything as profound as *re-inventing*, for God's sake, the *entire concept* of aging.

Maybe, knowing the Boomers, it's shallower than that. Maybe the poor babies simply can't accept the fact that they're now *twice as old* as the age they once disdained when they declared, "Never trust anyone over 30."

Yikes! Can it finally be happening? To *them*? Aren't they supposed to be immune from that . . . that . . . *ugliness*, that *helplessness*? Can they *really* be on the verge, after all those decades of being the hot shots, of getting that dreaded gold watch? Settling into that rocking chair to play cribbage and doze off in the afternoon, just like their parents and grandparents did, waiting for the Big Sleep?

No! No! It can't be!

So they pretend it away.

Isn't that what's really happening?

Well, yes, you could make that case. It's not a bad argument — but it's wrong.

And I want to deal with why it's wrong — right here at the beginning — because it enables me lay out a sort of Grand Theory of the whole ball game, a context in which you can place everything that follows.

What we're seeing is a lot more than the simple application of Boomer vanity to a new stage of life. We're seeing the confluence of many other forces. No one of them, on its own — not even the awful Boomer self-aggrandizement that drives Paul Begala nuts — would be strong enough to drive a process as big, and as lasting, as the one I'm describing. But put them all together, and the effect is irresistible. BoomerAging is happening because all of these forces are operating at the *same time, in more or less the same place.*

We can express it in a very simple diagram, as seen on the opposite page.

As the diagram shows, some of the forces are concrete — advances in medicine and technology, demography — and some of the forces are cultural or attitudinal. It is certainly possible to draw other versions of the diagram, and to list other forces. But I think the diagram does capture the essentials of what's going on. Let's take a quick look at each factor.

1. Boomer attitudes

It makes sense that the "Me" generation is going to resist — as strongly as possible — letting old age turn them into a generation of quiet, passive, helpless "seniors." Boomers grew up determined to experience new things, break new ground, get what they wanted. They see no reason to let their chronological age determine their mental or emotional age.

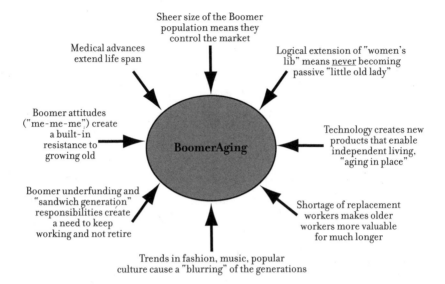

Fig. 2 — Cravit's Grand Theory: the confluence of forces that are making BoomerAging irresistible.

2. Logical extension of "women's lib"

The "going-in" attitudes of the Boomers are particularly revolutionary as far as women are concerned. The generation that pioneered "women's lib" has no intention of reverting to Pleasantville just because they've hit menopause. The dutiful "little woman" of the Eisenhower era (who had no choice but to accept it when hubby ran off with a sweet young thing) is a creature of the past. Today's Boomer women are more likely to be the partner who initiates a divorce, and they definitely see themselves as social, career and sexual "players" — possibly for decades to come.

3. Medical advancements = much longer life span

Just in time for the oldest Boomers to be hitting their 60s, medicine is giving 60-year-olds a better than 50% shot at . . . 90! And who knows what might be on the threshold of possibility? All of a sudden, a five-to-ten-year "retirement" — and then lights out — has turned into two or three more decades (if not more) of . . . what? Sitting around doing nothing?

4. Impact of technology making aging less onerous

Along with medical advances has come new technology — products and services that make aging more comfortable and convenient. The age at which you can't really be helped any longer, by either medicine or technology, is being pushed out further and further. If it's physically less stressful to be "older," then it automatically becomes easier to continue to think, feel and act "younger" for longer.

5. Need for the Boomers to keep working

But all isn't rosy. Despite the fact that they account for more than half of consumer wealth and almost half of consumer spending, the Boomers have huge expenses. They're the "sandwich generation," after all, taking care of both parents and children (and, in many cases, grandchildren), all at the same time. What's more, they grew up in an era that encouraged debt (in part because of high inflation) and discouraged savings. So they're seriously underfunded. Most of them are in no position to take that gold watch and see their income vanish at age 65. Stay active? Sure — *they have no choice.*

6. Need for the market to keep the Boomers working

The Boomers are lucky, though. (Yet again.) Just as they *need* to keep working, the economy *needs* them to do just that. There's a serious shortage of replacement workers coming up behind them. What's more, corporations are beginning to recognize the serious erosion of their competitive positions if the Boomers leave and take all their knowledge and experience with them. So businesses need to keep them in the workforce longer — and this in turn is gradually making the "older worker" a more familiar and accepted sight . . . which in turn reinforces all the other forces in play.

7. "Blurring" of the generations

At the same time as all this is happening, social and cultural trends — music, fashion, leisure — have been promoting a "blurring" of the generations, so that the pieces are more interchangeable than ever before. Ignoring a few extremes like hip-hop attire, "older" people and "younger" people wear substantially the same clothes. Boomers and their children listen to the same music — or at least, share many of the same favorites even if they also branch off into their own tastes. The Boomers have always been tech-savvy (a fact of which the advertising and marketing communities appear to be utterly unaware) and have embraced the Internet enthusiastically. So in most aspects of social and cultural behavior, there is less likelihood than ever before of a clear demarcation of "old" behavior and "younger" behavior.

8. Sheer size of the market

Take all of the above, and then factor in the sheer size of the Boomer population. It means that whatever the Boomers are doing, every other age group and every other aspect of society is being affected.

The Baby Boom has often been depicted as a rock traveling down the body of a snake. The snake is the total population, and the bulge represented by the rock is the age that the Baby Boomers have hit at that particular point in time. Because the Boomers have always been the largest single group, their concerns (and the demand for products that they represented) have always dominated the social, political and marketing agendas — the child and teen culture of the 1950s and early 1960s, which became the college-age protest movement, which morphed into the anti–Vietnam War movement, which morphed into the hippies, who became the money-driven yuppies of the 1970s, and so on. Today, the rock is approaching the tail end of the snake:

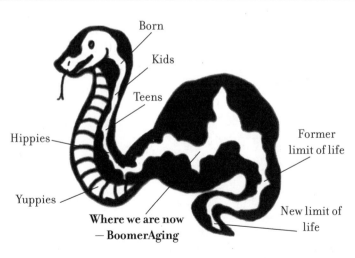

Born
Kids
Teens
Hippies
Yuppies
Where we are now — BoomerAging
Former limit of life
New limit of life

Fig. 3 — The rock moves through the snake as the Baby Boomers age.

Not surprisingly, then, the Boomers' agenda — BoomerAging — has become the most important force in society.

But, to repeat: it wouldn't be that way on the strength of Boomer attitudes alone. After all, if most people still died at 65, it wouldn't matter how badly the Boomers wanted to keep on looking and acting young. They'd have only a handful of years to do it in — which would probably make it a grotesque performance, at best — and then they'd be gone, six feet under, just like all previous generations.

So it's more than Boomer narcissism at work here. The narcissism, if you insist it's really there, is simply the filter through which the Boomers respond to all the other factors. It's "all of the above" — coming together at the same point in time — that is driving the phenomenon of BoomerAging.

Which is exactly why the phenomenon is unstoppable.

That's the big picture.

Now let's start looking at the details . . . and what to do about them.

CHAPTER 2   **Is Mick Jagger a senior citizen?**

Is Mick Jagger a senior citizen?

According to the British government, yes . . . absolutely.

Mick turned 64 in July of 2007. He's already four years into eligibility for a host of over-60 benefits offered by the UK government, including the Senior Railcard (save up to a third on the costs of train travel), various pension credits, a Cold Weather Payment and Winter Fuel Supplement to help with heating costs, and free travel on local buses during off-peak hours.

Now I'm not trying to make fun of all these wonderful benefits, just because Mick Jagger obviously doesn't need them. I'm just asking you to respond — quickly, *instinctively* — to the juxtaposition of *Mick Jagger* and *senior citizen*.

Doesn't it just plain "feel" wrong?

Isn't there an immediate disconnect?

Let's make it even more vivid.

Here are the photos of four people, taken when each of them had already passed their 60th birthday. Take a good look and tell me who is "old" and who isn't.

My grandfather, Isaac Kravitz, at age 65   *Mick Jagger at age 63*   *My grandmother, Sarah Lappin, at age 64*   *Diane Keaton at age 62*

Okay, the ages don't line up precisely. But is there any danger that Mick Jagger will begin to look like Isaac Kravitz in two more years, or that if I impose two more years on Diane Keaton she'll suddenly turn into Sarah Lappin?

For the record, my grandfather, Isaac Kravitz, went on to live for 30 more years after that photo was taken. My grandmother, Sarah Lappin, lived to 81. They both reached an age that would be considered "old" even today . . . Isaac particularly.

But the point is, they were already "old" when those photos were taken. "Old" in their early to mid-60s. *And nothing changed after that.* Though they went on living for many more years, and their bodies of course continued to age, their "oldness" was already fixed and frozen. It was simply a happy fluke that they spent many more years being "old" than the majority of their contemporaries who didn't live past their 70s. But the number of years of life had almost nothing to do with the degree of "oldness." They just kept on being "old" until the end.

The "oldness" I am describing is a combination of attitudes, habits and behaviors — experienced by the "old folks" themselves, and expected by their children and grandchildren. The table on the next page summarizes the key characteristics.

Of course, there have always been people for whom these "rules" did not apply, but I think, overall, the list is fair.

It's certainly true that almost everyone back then "retired" by age 65, and plans for the future were, to put it mildly, not robust. Even today the Canadian government still uses the "old age" tag to apply to pensions — *Old Age* Security (OAS), which kicks in at age 65. (In a later chapter, I'll have much more to say about how clueless governments are as to what's really happening out there.) Being "old" meant the active part of your life was over. You were stuck with whatever you had, good or bad. Being "old" meant *stopping*. The word *retirement* itself is very revealing, isn't it? It essentially means withdrawing, removing one's self from a situation or set of circumstances. You were supposed to "slow down" now, "take things easy" (a euphemism for doing more or less nothing), and somehow "enjoy" this passivity.

To Isaac Kravitz, the idea of "re-inventing himself" and trying something entirely new, would have been literally incomprehensible.

1. Work is over	When you are "old," you retire and receive your old age pension. You never go back to work again.
2. Planning for the future is over	When you are "old," there's no sense making any plans for the future, because you don't have much of a future.
3. Sex is over . . .	. . . or at least, never acknowledged (particularly for women).
4. Brand choices and shopping habits are set in stone	When you are "old," you're no longer interested in trying new products. You stick to the brands you already know and use. As a result, you're not really worth marketing to.
5. The modern world is engaged only slightly	When you are "old," your involvement with the "modern world" is peripheral. You may keep up with the news, and you may know how to use some of the newfangled products (e.g., TV), but basically you're just an observer, not an active user.

Table 2 — Characteristics of "oldness" as experienced by Isaac Kravitz and Sarah Lappin — and every generation before BoomerAging created the New Old

As for sex, it's true that we all grew up with the cliché of the "dirty old man." And there is, indeed, a hilarious family legend about Isaac Kravitz, at 90, getting it on with an 85-year-old woman from the old folks' home (note the name).

But that's the whole point . . . it was hilarious precisely because it was an aberration, something you never heard about. For the most part, "old" meant sex was over — particularly for women. Take another look at the Diane Keaton picture. She's currently the spokesperson for the L'Oréal Paris line of Age Perfect skin care products — specifically targeting women in their 50s and 60s. Now imagine Sarah Lappin as a potential customer. It just doesn't work, does it?

The rigidity of brand choices and shopping habits was another safe assumption back then. If you were "old," you were no longer interested in trying new products (except, possibly, for a tiny range of health-related products that you had never needed previously . . . like false teeth). Your brand of toothpaste, your brand of coffee, your brand of breakfast cereal, the car you drove (if you were still driving), the cigarettes you smoked (because who knew, back then?) . . . those tastes had all been formed back in your 20s and 30s and maybe, when you made a few more bucks, your 40s. And nothing was going to change them now.

This truth became frozen, in the minds of marketers and their ad agencies, and still governs much of their attitudes and actions today . . . helping to explain why the marketing industry is so far behind in understanding and responding to the BoomerAging phenomenon.

No more work, no more big plans, no more sex, no more experimentation in the marketplace — it all added up to a passivity to, if not outright detachment from, the "modern world."

My grandfather Isaac Kravitz was born in a tiny village in the Ukraine — so backward, he used to tell us, that when he was a boy and a group of young strangers passed through one day on bicycles, the whole town turned out to see it. He lived to watch Neil Armstrong step onto the moon. Yet by his early 60s, "oldness" had set in — and he made little or no effort to understand, or engage, new products, new ideas, new possibilities. Of course he could drive a car and turn on the TV (he loved wrestling), but he remained essentially unengaged, an observer, certainly aware of what was out there, but rarely able to see how it had much to do with him. After all, he could be dead soon, couldn't he? So for over 30 years he remained "old."

It could be argued, of course, that some of this stemmed from the fact that he was from "the Old Country" (and thus, somewhat alienated from the North American "modernity" all along), and that it was this reality — rather than his "oldness" — that inhibited him from really being engaged. And, certainly, I have friends and associates from other "Old Country" backgrounds (particularly Italian) who report the same reactions (or lack of reactions) on the part of their own grandparents.

So, yes, that may explain part of it. Yet I have also observed exactly the same thing in the UK, among people who were living where they had been born and brought up.

In my early 20s, I lived in London and worked as a newspaper reporter for a suburban community weekly. I often covered church events, events at the "old people's home" and other places where you could find significant numbers of the "older generation." And I witnessed the same kind of disconnect from the "modern" world. It wasn't that they didn't know about new products, better technology, or even new sociopolitical ideas and trends. It was that they approached these things more or less as passive *observers*, and not with any strong desire to embrace, to engage, to exploit what was new in order to benefit from it. After all, being "old," how much difference could it make to them? And for how long? Of course there were individual differences — some were more interested, some a little bolder, some more tenuous or even frightened, some adapted not too badly, some grudgingly, some not at all . . . but in the end, they were essentially just watching the parade.

Today, led by the Boomers, they feel like they *are* the parade. Boomer-Aging is reversing each of the characteristics of "oldness" that governed all previous generations.

The Old Old	**The New Old**
Work is over	Work goes on (and a whole new career may be just beginning)
Planning for the future is over	Planning for the future is active, and may take you in surprising new directions
Sex is over	Sex is never over
Brand choices and shopping habits are set in stone	There is no brand loyalty; everything is up for grabs
The modern world is engaged only slightly	The modern world is still a playground, and guess who's the boss

Table 3 – The end of "oldness." How BoomerAging has wiped out the attitudes and behaviors of previous generations, converting The Old Old to The New Old

BoomerAging has changed everything.

Retirement? The Boomers not only don't want to retire, for the most part they can't afford to. This reality sets off a chain reaction of new attitudes and behaviors, as well as new mechanisms to enable the Boomers to keep working — and new challenges to long-established government policies regarding retirement, pensions and other benefits for the "elderly."

Planning for the future? The Boomers are operating from the assumption that they have 25 or 30 years left (or maybe even longer.) Plenty of time not only to plan for the future, but to envision a whole series of futures. They're starting new businesses, going back to school, traveling around the world, entering into new relationships, constantly churning, "re-inventing" themselves.

Sex? This one is obvious. More — much more — later.

Brand choices and shopping habits? Puh-leeze. If the Boomers were clinging only to the brand they grew up with, Ipana would still be an important toothpaste. The fact is, Boomers are no more brand loyal than younger consumers — and unlike younger consumers, they have actual money.

So, unlike people of previous generations at this same age, the Boomers are *thoroughly* engaged with the modern world. In fact, in many ways they finally *rule* the modern world. They embrace technology readily — after all, 20-some years ago they were the yuppies who had to own every possible toy. They eagerly search for new knowledge and new products — especially those that can keep them living even longer.

But they don't just participate, they're shaping the whole ball game — just as they've done their whole lives. Their purchasing power rules the marketplace. Their voting power is starting to push their agendas to the head of the line. One last thumb in the eye of Boomer-haters like Paul Begala — one more flexing of the muscles before the lights go out. And why not? That's who Boomers are; that's what they do.

Elizabeth Debold puts it well in her review of the novel *Boomeritis:*

I am a boomer. Blooming right in the middle of the boomer era — born in 1955 — and still booming strong. I have been part of one paradigm-busting, revolutionary movement after another since I came of age in the early seventies . . . I know that whatever I'm involved in has the potential to entirely transform the world as we know it, to free us from the untold horrors of, well, you name it — patriarchy, racism, class oppression. Why? Because I'm a boomer, and boomers are going to change the world.

BoomerAging may be the most profound change the Boomers have ever engineered — because its effects will be felt long after the Boomers are gone. In fact, there's already a spillover — *upward* — to the people who are 10–15 years older than the Boomers.

Today we're hearing that "60 is the new 40." Maybe someday it will be "100 is the new 60." It's an efficient way of dealing with aging; you simply define it away.

This was driven home to me very vividly in a focus group we conducted a few months ago, as part of the ongoing research we do at ZoomerMedia into the attitudes and behaviors of our audience. We were talking to a group of people, the youngest of whom was 60 and the oldest 73. We asked them, simply, "What do you consider 'old'?"

They all settled — quickly and without much discussion — on the same number: 85.

"So you don't consider yourself old?" we asked the 73-year-old.

"Who, me? Old? No, I'm not old. I'm not saying I'm *young*, mind you. But old? No, no — old is 85 . . . maybe 87."

To this point, I've been leading you pretty firmly through the argument that says "oldness" is no more:

· It's been re-defined so as to start later and later.
· And even once its appearance is acknowledged, a whole new set of attitudes, expectations and behaviors are replacing the previous characteristics that were attached to it.

And I've offered a short and simple name for what's happening: BoomerAging.

So is that it?

Everyone either pretends they're not old or willfully acts younger than their years? End of story?

Not quite.

Not even the Boomers can literally go backward in time. They can think, feel and act younger — but every 365 days they have to add another year to their age.

How do you grow older and stay younger at the same time? *You do both.* In a very real sense, the Boomers are the first *multi-age* generation, living at several different ages simultaneously.

The Boomer mindset starts by seeing oneself as 10–15 years younger than one's chronological age. Attitude, behavior and expectations stay young, in part denying what is happening, in part re-defining it out of existence, in part glorying in establishing new norms and patterns so that the traditional "oldness" stereotypes are shattered.

But the body does age, and this gradually imposes certain physical constraints, and the need to take preventative or remedial action. Aging also brings with it more knowledge and experience, enabling the Boomers to look at everything both through the prism of a younger-than-their-age *attitude*, and an at-their-age *wisdom*.

Thus the Boomer has a foot in both camps, "younger" and "older." The Boomer is an amalgam of different ages, and different age-related attitudes and drives, all co-existing — and jockeying for position — in the same individual at the same time. This is the "side effect," if you will, of Boomer-Aging — and as we will see, it makes for a very interesting and challenging customer.

A 60-year-old Boomer, for example, feels and acts like he is still 45. But if you put him in a room full of actual 45-year-olds, there would be at least one obvious, and very important, difference. The Boomer would have 15 more years of experience than the others. He'd have bought two or three more cars, flipped one or two more houses, seen at least one extra boom/bust cycle that the younger people hadn't witnessed. He couldn't *un-know* what he's seen, what he's experienced and what he knows (and what the others in the room don't know). Yes, he's thinking and acting younger than his years — but he's also carrying the knowledge and experience (and problems) of the age he's reached.

Thus there's a disconnect, in a sense — or at least a complication in the relationship — between his chronological age and his attitudinal age.

But both drive him; both create attitudes, expectations, behaviors and constraints. He must respond to both, at the same time.

To illustrate how this "split personality" works, let's look at some Boomer composites. I've created four examples, and I think you'll find them all very recognizable.

BILL SMITH, born in 1946
Disconnect #1 — Is 61, but acts 45
- *Starting a new career*
- *His "retirement" is seriously underfunded*
- *Runs three miles a day*
- *Technologically very capable*
- *Wears youthful fashion*

Disconnect #2 — Acts 45, but is 61
- *Has grandchildren*
- *Worried investor — has a lot of catching up to do*
- *Takes longer to recover from runs than his younger jogging buddies*
- *Chooses loose-fitting jeans*

JILL McDONALD, born in 1962
Disconnect #1 — Is 45, but acts 33
- *Physically active — has just taken up snowboarding*
- *Has just started a new retail business*
- *Recently separated — is back on the dating scene (and spending a ton of money to keep herself looking young)*

Disconnect #2 — Acts 33, but is 45
- *Only goes on easier hills when boarding because she realizes that if injured, she would heal more slowly than she would have ten years ago*
- *Cautious about the new business — isn't putting all her money into it*
- *Realistic about dating — targeting men in their late 40s to late 50s*

MIKE DIFRANCO, born in 1957
Disconnect #1 — Is 50, but acts 35
- *Rides a Harley Davidson*
- *Shops on the Internet*
- *Wears youthful fashion*
- *Taking online courses in order to "re-invent" himself in a new business*

Disconnect #2 — Acts 35, but is 50
- *Has had a heart attack*
- *Worried about his weight and cholesterol — is experimenting with "longevity" diets*
- *Won't buy a new car because his 9-year-old car is still doing fine*

SUSAN DOUGLAS, born in 1949
Disconnect #1 — Is 58, but acts 45
- *Still likes to party — dinner, dancing, the works!*
- *Works seven days a week as a real estate agent, keeping up a frantic pace*
- *Spend a lot of money on holidays and fixing up the house, but not as much on retirement savings*

Disconnect #2 — Acts 45, but is 58
- *Can't handle alcohol like when she was younger, so drinks a glass of water between cocktails*
- *Worried investor, frantically trying to catch up on her under-funded retirement portfolio (but still not putting enough money in)*
- *Has grandchildren and often worries about her job preventing her from spending enough time with them*

It's immediately apparent that all of these folks are juggling often contradictory influences. But the balance is certainly tipped in favor of the youthful side: BoomerAging means *dragging with you* some of the unavoidable effects of aging, but not letting them stop you from maintaining more youthful attitudes, expectations and experiences. BoomerAging means pushing back against labels that nudge you toward "oldness."

The examples I've given are all, technically, Baby Boomers. Bill Smith, the oldest, was born in 1946, one year into the Baby Boom in the USA and the kick-off year in Canada. Jill McDonald, the youngest, was born near the tail end of the Baby Boom, in 1962.

But what about people a year or two *older* than Bill Smith? Obviously they don't automatically revert to the Isaac Kravitz version of "oldness." How about five years older than Bill? Ten?

The BoomerAging process, while driven by the Boomers, spills into the older age brackets too. As we will see, people in their mid- to late-60s have discarded "oldness" in much the same way Boomers have. And the influence can be seen in some areas — such as fashion, health and beauty, leisure, housing — right up into the 70- and even 80-year-old brackets.

There's been an interesting vacuum, in marketing circles, as to just what to call this population.

"Seniors" — the traditional designation — is becoming increasingly unacceptable. (Leave it to the government, like that of the province of

Ontario, to create a Seniors' Secretariat just in time for nobody to want to be called a "senior" anymore!). I've had 75-year-olds tell me they don't want to be called "seniors."

There are several problems with the word.

First, it's imprecise. It's been most frequently applied to people over the age of 65, but sometimes over 60, or even over 50.

Worse, it carries with it an unmistakable tinge of patronization — what I call the "There, there, dear" syndrome. When you hear "senior citizen" — let's face it — you immediately think of all the characteristics of "oldness" that we were talking about earlier.

Worse still, with the dramatic increases in life span, the label is starting to attach itself to way too many people.

Susan J. Ellis expressed this well in an article entitled "Don't Call Me A Senior!" (April 2002) on www.energize.com:

> The fastest growing age range in developed countries is now ages 90 to 100. If we begin considering people age 55 (Senior Corps) or even 50 (AARP) to be "seniors," we are applying that label to an age cohort spanning 50+ years. One could be considered a "senior" for fully half of one's lifetime! I have said before that I think our vocabulary fails us when it comes to talking about age. We really need new words to discuss the younger senior (perhaps 60–75), the middle senior (75–85?), and the older senior (85+).

I particularly like the part about being considered a "senior" for half of your lifetime. But it's not so far-fetched. Over 50,000 Americans are 100 or older. Even if only 5,000 of them were members of AARP (and overall, AARP has about a 30% share of the total 50-plus population), it means they've spent half their life labeled as a "senior."

No, thanks.

We must think of something else.

Jack Rosenthal dealt with this issue in an interesting column in *The New York Times* in July 2007. "Harry (Rick) Moody, a scholar on the subject of aging, describes the great majority as the wellderly, distinct from the afflicted illderly," Rosenthal wrote. "But that witty distinction doesn't solve the larger nomenclature problem. Language has not yet caught up with life." Exactly.

"No variation of elderly encompasses the vast variety and abilities of people over 55 or 65," Rosenthal goes on. "Yet we keep looking for a single generic term. Oldsters and golden agers are patronizing, targets for comics . . . An earlier generation found senior citizens acceptable, and senior as an adjective, as in senior vice-president, remains so. But not as a noun, as in seniors." What to do? "The ultimate answer will most likely be a suite of functional and factual terms, like the typology scholars use to distinguish between the young old, 65 to 80; the old old, 80 to 90; the oldest old 90 to 99; and centenarians. Terms like these, though somewhat awkward, are apt to enter common usage as society faces up to the new age of age. Necessity is the mother of locution."

The best label was invented by my boss, Moses Znaimer, Canada's foremost media innovator. Moses has always been decades ahead of the curve. He was envisioning specialty TV channels over 40 years ago, and he has created a succession of breakthrough stations and formats, including CityTV, MuchMusic, Bravo!, Space, Fashion Television and more.

Moses has identified the Boomers and "seniors" as the next hottest market, and in late 2007 he became the majority shareholder of Zoomer-Media, the company I work for. Nobody understands this market — and where it's going — better than he does, because he has been, in a very real sense, the leader of the Baby Boomers' media tastes all along, and he is now taking them to the next phase.

Moses was born in 1942, so he's technically a couple of years older than the oldest Boomers. "In that sense, I'm the scout," he said in an October 2007 interview in *The Globe and Mail.* "I go ahead, I suss out the terrain, I take some of those early risks and I bring the report back, and the report is that we're into this cataclysmic change in human life."

Moses popularized the term "Zoomers" (Boomers with zip) to describe this market, and presents himself — quite accurately, I believe — as the archetype.

The term is ideal because it perfectly conveys the sense of *action* that, above all, characterizes BoomerAging. No matter what the chronological age, for the Zoomer there is no *retirement*, there is only engagement: more experiences, more discovery . . . more spending!

It's not only that the Zoomer is the sum of all of the ages he or she has ever lived through — it's that *all those ages are still in operation, all at the same time.*

- Body of a 65-year-old
  Well, okay, the body is what it is. But as we'll see, there is a ferocious battle to keep that body healthier and more active for as long as possible — and an increasing array of products and services to make that battle a successful one.

- Mind of a 45-year-old
  The Boomers — stretched to *Zoomers* — always see themselves as 10–15 years younger than their chronological age.

- Libido of a 25-year-old
Sex has always been important, so why should it fall off the radar screen now?

- Heart of a teenager
Passion, a constant interest in new experiences, and even, as we'll see, the idea that death isn't ever going to happen.

- Controls the spending
The kicker . . . and the real reason marketers, policy-makers, academics and the media are finally starting to wake up to BoomerAging. Zoomers spend more money, in just about every category, than all the other age groups combined.

The Zoomer, as described by Moses Znaimer, can be seen as the "end product" of BoomerAging: the clock keeps ticking, but the body resists, the mind and spirit resist even harder, and so a whole new collection of attitudes, expectations and behaviors comes into play.

In early 2008, Moses held a press conference to introduce the Zoomer idea, and to announce some of the ways he would be bringing this concept to life. Our company was rebranded as ZoomerMedia (its former name was Fifty-Plus.Net International Inc.). CARP's magazine — previously called, duh, CARP — was to be rebranded as Zoomer Magazine, and Canada's foremost editor, fashion icon Suzanne Boyd, was recruited to be editor-in-chief. A communications campaign targeting ad agencies, media buyers and marketing executives, was packaged as an online "virtual university" (www.uofz.ca), complete with a Latin motto that summed up the entire Zoomer ethos: *Cori. Menti. Libidos. Argenti.* (Hearts. Minds. Libidos. Money.)

"We all want to live a long time — nobody wants to be old," Moses said. "Old is not a good word, and variations on the concept of old make people squirm, especially since we came out of a culture that wildly overemphasized youth, so we have an entire generation that is kind of programmed to resist the concept of age. Zoomer is a word people can instantly identify with. It has a certain drive, it has a certain optimism, and the very same people who will never reveal their age are pleased to self-identify as Zoomers."

Within hours, the word Zoomer was everywhere in the media. It was even on Wikipedia.

There was no question that Moses had struck a very powerful chord with the Zoomer idea. Less than a month after the initial press conference,

Moses Znaimer unveils new look
for 50-plus group dubbed 'Zoomer' generation

CanadianPress.com
Feb 28th, 2008

TORONTO - As the media mastermind behind the country's first specialty music cable channel, **Moses Znaimer** had his sights squarely focused on capturing the attention of Canada's youth.

Now the broadcasting innovator who brought **MuchMusic** and **Citytv** to the masses is hoping to employ an all-encompassing multimedia strategy to reach out and connect with an older generation.

Znaimer is the new executive director of **CARP**, Canada's Association for the Fifty Plus. In December, the media mogul completed a transaction that consolidated Kemur Publishing and http://www.Fifty-Plus.Net International Inc., which included gaining media associated with CARP, like its eponymous magazine, websites and online publishing assets.

At a news conference Thursday held at **Classical 96.3 FM** - one of two radio stations Znaimer chairs - he unveiled his vision to bring a fresh look and voice to the organization and its target 50-plus age demographic.

He's even coined a name to describe the age group representing more than 14 million Candians - **"Zoomers,"** a term he says combines the word "boomer" with the concepts of "vitality and zip."

"We all want to live a long time - nobody wants to be old," Znaimer said in an interview. "Old is not a good word, and variations on the concept of old make people squirm, especially since we came out of a culture that wildly overemphasized youth, so we have an entire generation that is kind of programmed to resist the concept of age."

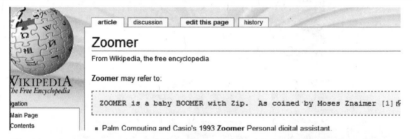

| article | discussion | edit this page | history |

Zoomer

From Wikipedia, the free encyclopedia

Zoomer may refer to:

ZOOMER is a baby BOOMER with Zip. As coined by Moses Znaimer [1]

- Palm Computing and Casio's 1993 **Zoomer** Personal digital assistant.

Welcome to U of Z

Enrol Today!
U of Z Registration Form

First Name

Last Name

Title

Company

City

Province
-- Select Province --

Email

Password (5 - 12 characters)

All fields are required
[Send Registration]

PRESIDENT'S
Message

Even though we think we live in a knowledge-based age, misleading "common wisdom" can sometimes maintain its grip on our psyche -- even in the face of overwhelming evidence to the contrary.

One such idea is that Zoomers are old and retired and set in their ways.

To dispel this misguided notion, I founded U of Z.

U of Z is the only virtual university dedicated to Zoomers. This web site will provide a constant flow of information and research, to educate marketing professionals and to help them more effectively reach the largest demographic with the most money and the

YOU COULD *Win!*
an All-Expense Paid Trip for 2

ENROL NOW -- IT'S FREE...
AND YOU'RE AUTOMATICALLY
ENTERED TO WIN A 5 NIGHT GOLF
AND SPA TRIP TO LA QUINTA
RESORT AND CLUB IN PALM
SPRINGS, CALIFORNIA

Courtesy Of:

merit
GOLF VACATIONS

he was featured on the cover of *Marketing*, the magazine that covers Canada's advertising and marketing industry. The cover perfectly captures the impact of what Moses Znaimer had done.

Within a few months, the term was being routinely used in the media. In fact, many writers no longer felt it necessary to explain where the term had come from; it was assumed that the reader knew and accepted the term as the way to define this demographic. For example, a restaurant review criticized the music being played at a Toronto restaurant because "Zoomers wouldn't like it." The word is rapidly becoming a word you use like Kleenex (which doesn't exactly hurt our company, or Moses Znaimer's reputation for insight and innovation).

Even more important than the media uptake, has been the reaction of the Zoomers themselves. As noted in the previous chapter, CARP rebranded itself as "Canada's Association for Zoomers," and members eagerly adapted the term. We've been inundated by letters, phone calls and e-mails celebrating the new word. After all, who wouldn't prefer to think of themselves — and be thought of by others — as a Zoomer, instead of as a "senior"?

At ZoomerMedia, we use the term to encompass both the Baby Boomers and everyone older. (For a more detailed explanation and a collection of Zoomer stats, see Chapter 8 or check our websites at www.zoomermedia.ca or www.uofz.ca.)

But it's really the Baby Boomers, and how they are — and are not — aging, who are the first movers here, setting the pace, shattering "oldness" for good. Is there any chance that those who are younger than the Boomers — that is, under the age of 45 — will revert to the way things were before the Boomers came along? Of course not — the next generation will be living longer still. A baby girl born in North America while you were reading this chapter has a 50% chance of reaching her 100th birthday — and that's with *today's* level of medical and scientific advancement. By the time she gets her university degree — let's say at age 22 — she could be looking at — never mind another 75 years of life — but a further *century* of life! What happens to the concepts of education, family, career and retirement then?

This is why BoomerAging is so important. It's not just a moderate trend, an interesting development affecting a particular segment of the population — it's a pervasive and *permanent* shattering of all past ideas of the human life span. It's a re-definition what aging is, what it means and how to deal with it — and by extension, it demands a re-thinking of virtually every aspect of how our society operates.

Much of that re-thinking, as we'll see, is already well underway. So let's start looking at the specifics.

PART TWO: THE NEW OLD LANDSCAPE

CHAPTER 3 **Back to Methuselah**

The first big factor driving BoomerAging is the simple fact that life expectancy is increasing . . . and dramatically.

As with so many other phases of their lives, the Boomers again strike it lucky. Their mental attitude was *always* that the music must never stop, and now, just in time for it to matter, along comes longevity that previous generations couldn't have imagined.

Let's deal with some of the basic numbers right away.

First, let's look at life expectancy at birth. The chart below shows the numbers for Canada, the USA and the UK in 1900 and in 2000. In all three countries, life expectancy at birth was *under 50* in 1900; a century later, it was about 80.

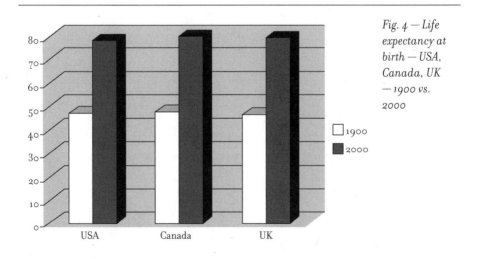

Fig. 4 — Life expectancy at birth — USA, Canada, UK — 1900 vs. 2000

☐ 1900
■ 2000

So life expectancy at birth jumped almost 60% in the 20th century —
an incredible advance never seen before.

To put it in perspective, life expectancy at birth in the Middle Ages was
about 35. So it took mankind over 500 years to add *just 15 years* to life expectancy at birth — but then another 30 years was added in the 20th century
alone.

But life expectancy at birth is only part of the story. The average is
dragged down, obviously, by all the people who die young. What's the
outlook if you make it to 65?

In 1900, those over the age of 65 represented just 4.1% of the US population, and could look forward to an average of 12 more years. In 2000,
they represented 12.4% of the US population, and could look forward to 18
more years, on average — a 50% increase from 1900.

But it isn't just the total number of extra years that's impressive — it's
the accelerating rate of that gain. Take a look at this chart:

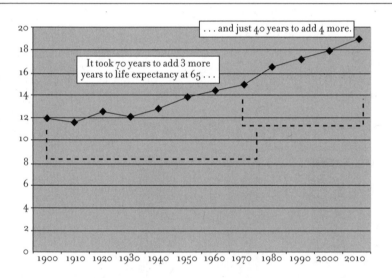

Fig. 5 — Life expectancy at age 65, USA, 1900–2010

As the chart shows, a 65-year-old in 1900 had 12 more years of life expectancy. It took 70 years to get this number up to 15. So that was a 33% jump
in the life expectancy of a 65-year-old — and seven decades to achieve it.

But now comes a further 33% jump — to almost 20 more years of life — and it will have been accomplished in 40 years, not 70.

Similar patterns apply in Canada and the UK — 11 more years of a life for a 65-year-old in 1900, about 18 more years today . . . and rising fast.

And all these numbers, of course, are averages. A significant number of people will exceed those averages. For a married couple who are both 65 today, there's a 50% chance that one of them will reach the age of 92.

There are solid reasons for the increased longevity in the USA, Canada and most of Western Europe — reasons that go deeper than the "forever young" attitude of the Boomers.

As the Center for Disease Control has documented, the 20th century saw steady *decreases* in the number of deaths from stroke and heart attacks, particularly after World War II:

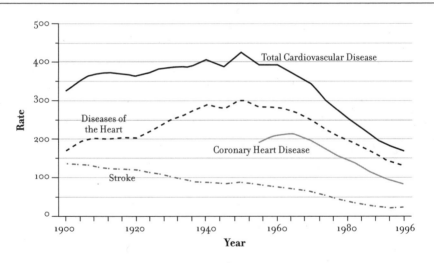

Fig. 6 — Death rate per 100,000, USA, 1900–2010

The dramatic improvements were due to many factors, including:

· Successful public health campaigns to reduce smoking
· A decrease in mean blood pressures and an increase in the number of people with hypertension who had the condition treated and controlled

- Improvements in diet, including decreases in the consumption of saturated fats and cholesterol
- Continuing improvements in medical care, including advances in diagnosis and treatment of heart disease and stroke, better medications, improved emergency room services, more coronary care units

The same observations could be made about cancer — healthier habits, better diagnosis, improved medical care and, in particular, breakthroughs in drug therapy have all contributed to a consistent lowering of the death rates.

So even if the Boomers weren't obsessed with staying young, the overall "health environment" is giving them more years. And the *rate* of that increase shows no signs of slowing down, especially given the potential of gene therapy and other medical breakthroughs of which there seem to be a never-ending supply.

But of course, being the Boomers, they can't just leave it at that.

They have to push — and are pushing — for even more.

Longevity? Why stop there? How about *immortality*?

Here's an excerpt from the introduction to *The Baby Boomer's Guide to Living Forever*, by Terry Grossman, MD, published in 2000 by the aptly named Hubristic Press:

> I believe I am more intrigued with the idea of living forever than with such a reality. As an official member of the Baby Boomer generation, I really and truly do not believe that it was intended for us to die. Death, if and when it occurs, clearly will represent a mistake of some kind. While I am no official spokesperson for the Boomers, I feel I do accurately express the hubris of my generation. According to my interpretation of the master plan, the Baby Boomers will be the first generation ever to have the option of immortality.

Crazy? Tongue in cheek? The fantasies of a deluded egomaniac? It would be easy to dismiss it, to accuse me of having trolled the planet to come up with one egregious example of utter silliness. But it's not so. The quest for a longer and longer life span — for quantum leaps in life span, extending perhaps by centuries, if not more — is a serious one, and a significant number of people are pursuing it.

I'm not a scientist. I'm completely unqualified to judge how realistic the quest is, and if what is presented as new possibilities, backed up by hard science, is in fact real or rubbish. What counts, for our purposes, is not so much the immediate prospects of pushing the average life span toward 120 . . . 150 . . . and maybe a lot more, but, rather, the mere fact that the topic exists and can be spoken about with a straight face.

Here's just a small sampling.

We open with The Methuselah Institute and a foundation by the same name that claims we are on the threshold of increasing the human life span by *centuries*.

The chairman, Aubrey D. N. J. de Grey, holds a Ph.D. from Cambridge and works in the university's Department of Genetics, while also writing, lecturing and serving on the scientific advisory boards of numerous organizations whose names are unambiguous, to say the least: Supercente-narian Research Foundation, Maximum Life Foundation, Alcor Life Ex-tension Foundation, Immortality Institute, Singularity Institute for Artificial Intelligence, Foresight Institute . . . you get the idea.

In his online bio, Dr. de Grey states very straightforwardly, "The central goal of my work is to expedite the development of a true cure for human aging."

Dr. de Grey has pioneered a program called SENS — Strategies for En-gineered Negligible Senescence. Here's the description:

> SENS is a detailed plan for curing human aging. SENS is an engineering project, recognizing that aging is a medical condition and that medi-cine is a branch of engineering. Aging is a set of progressive changes in body composition, at the molecular and cellular level, which are side-effects of essential metabolic processes. Many of these changes are eventually bad for us — they are an accumulation of damage, which becomes pathogenic above a certain threshold of abundance.
>
> The traditional gerontological approach to life extension is to try to slow down this accumulation of damage. This is a misguided strategy. . . . An even more short-termist alternative is the geriatric approach, which is to try to stave off pathology in the face of accumulating damage; this is a losing battle because the continuing accumulation of damage makes pathology more and more inescapable.
>
> Instead, the engineering (SENS) strategy is not to interfere with the metabolism per se, but to repair or obviate the accumulating damage and thereby indefinitely postpone the age at which it reaches patho-genic levels. . . .

The website contains a neat little diagram that contrasts the ap-proaches of gerontology, geriatrics and engineering (SENS):

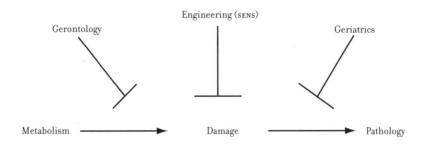

Fig. 7 — Alternative approaches to aging

"The strange arrows with flat heads," the website says, "are a notation used in the literature of gene expression and gene regulation, and they mean 'inhibits.' Thus, geriatrics is an attempt to stop damage from causing pathology; traditional gerontology is the attempt to stop metabolism from causing damage; and the SENS (engineering) approach is periodically to eliminate the damage, so keeping its abundance below the level that causes any pathology."

Thus, the "cure" for aging.

According to the website, components of the SENS strategy are "likely to be feasible in mice within a decade (presuming adequate funding), and may be translatable to humans within a decade or two thereafter."

Ah. The funding. Of course.

Here, the Methuselah organization has taken a very creative step. They're offering a prize — The Mouse Prize — to the researchers who develop the longest-living *mus musculus*, the breed of mouse most commonly used in research.

The logic is impeccable: "Developing interventions which work in mice is a critical precursor to the development of human anti-aging techniques, for once it is demonstrated that aging in mice can be effectively delayed or reversed, popular attitudes towards aging as 'inevitable' will no longer be possible."

The Foundation has also created The 300 (inspired by the 300 Spartans at Thermopylae), intended to be a group of donors who will pledge $1,000 a year for 25 years.

Thus far, the Foundation has raised millions of dollars toward the cause.

To repeat: I am not remotely qualified to judge the scientific validity — or the probability of success — of SENS and the Methuselah Foundation. It's fair to comment, though, that their credentials seem formidable, and there is a considerable amount of research, international conferencing and other tell-tale signs of legitimacy to the campaign.

And it's only one of many.

Here's the Immortality Institute (www.imminst.org), which publishes books, produces films, hosts conferences and runs online forums.

On the day I visited the website, the home page was featuring an excerpt from a book on *ending* aging. A brief fragment will give you a good idea of the viewpoint:

. . . many people alive today [will] live to 1,000 years of age and . . . avoid age-related health problems even at that age. It's a good explanation of the plausibility of *actuarial escape velocity*, the step by step process by which we could bootstrap our way to agelessness, one rejuvenation therapy at a time.

Actuarial escape velocity.

Has a nice, scientific ring to it, no? It suggests a kind of quiet inevitability, made more plausible by the very blandness of the terminology.

The concept was developed by David Gobel, a founder of . . . you guessed it . . . the Methusaleh Foundation. It envisions a time at which the rate of advance of biomedical technology exceeds the rate at which humans age, so that each year the average human life expectancy increases by a year or more.

How long will it take for that to happen? Nobody knows — but if you're worried it will take too long to do you any good, you can always try cryonics. Several organizations promote this technology; the one I checked out was Alcor Life Extension Foundation (www.alcor.org).

As the website explains, "Cryonics is the science of using ultra-cold temperatures to preserve human life with the intent of restoring good health when technology becomes available to do so."

Urban legend has had it that celebrities like Walt Disney and Ted Williams had either undergone the process or taken it seriously enough to make inquiries. Alcor claims 820 members and 76 "patients in cryopreservation."

I could go on and on with other theories, methodologies and organizations. To get an idea of just how big the topic is, let's go to Google and see.*

First, I enter the search phrase, "Staying young forever."

Almost two million results. Articles, books, blogs, products, tips, counterattacks . . . on and on and on it goes. Let's assume the relevancy of the Google results drops off enormously after we're 5% through the list. This still leaves 100,000 results for us to play with.

***Important note:** *Since this is the first of many Google searches I'll be showing you, let me insert my one big Google disclaimer right here. In no case have I actually waded through tens of thousands, let alone millions, of results to determine exactly where the relevancy of the search results approaches the vanishing point. In each case I'm simply showing you the first results screen and noting the declared total. As you will see, in all cases the number is immense. I concede that a more "scientific" search by a real expert in Google methodology, using quotation marks or other symbols to make the search more precise, would produce a lower number of results. But the real point is this: my Google searches involve terms or concepts that, in and of themselves, would have been unthinkable 10 or 15 years ago. So even if you were to rework the search terminology so as to cut my results in half — or more — you're still left with some scary totals.*

But let's face it, "staying young forever" is a hopeless task. The Boomers, for all that they're re-defining "old," are already no longer "young." A more realistic goal is the acceptance of the new version of aging (deny, delay, re-define) — while continuing to strive for a longer and longer life span . . . and, hey, as long as we're on the subject, why not immortality?

So we enter a new search term, one that is simpler, more modest, and more realistic than "staying young forever." Instead, we punch in, quite simply, "living forever."

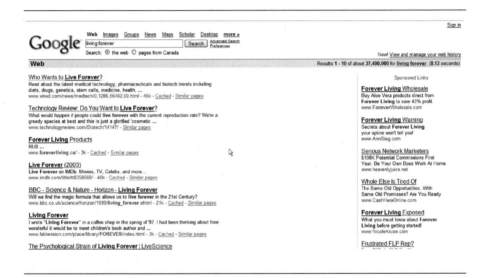

Now look what happens: almost *40 million* results. A 20-fold increase.

So what does all this prove?

Simply this — that it's out there.

It's being written about, being talked about — with a straight face, by thousands of people, not all of whom are delusional. We can laugh at the word "immortality," of course. We can snicker at the folks who are willing to pay tens of thousands of dollars to be frozen into a state of suspended animation, pending the arrival of as-yet-undiscovered medical technologies. But no matter how far we cut back the projections, no matter how ruthlessly we weed out anything but the most conservative forecasts, it's evident that we are on the threshold of even more dramatic increases in life expectancy — well past 110, possibly past 150. Which, for the purposes of my line of argument, is more than enough.

Because what counts, of course, is the *perception* of what is possible. This is what drives the behavior of the Boomers. It is already quite reasonable for the average Boomer, assuming he/she is still in reasonably good health, to expect to live to 90. It is tantalizingly possible — if the Boomer can buy another 10 or 15 years — to envision living to 110 or maybe 120. Or at least, there is enough "respectable" buzz around such a target to make it plausible.

So the youngest Boomers, at 44, can be looking at 70 more years of life. They're only a little more than a third of the way through.

And the oldest Boomers, at 62, can be looking at 40 or 50 or maybe, if they can hang in until some Methuselah-like breakthroughs, 60 more years of life. They can be drinking a toast — as I and my two closest friends did on our 60th birthdays — "to a great second half."

Now it doesn't really matter if these expectations are actually achieved. It matters only that they *are* expectations, and that there is just enough evidence to make them plausible (which there certainly is). Because it is the *expectation* that triggers everything else.

If I'm 65 and it's 1950 and I perceive I have maybe a decade or so of life remaining, then a number of attitudes and behaviors follow fairly automatically:

- Objectively, I'm "old." I have lived almost 85% of my life.
- Therefore, I think and act "old."
- I don't have enough time left to make, much less carry out, dramatic new plans. There's no question of "re-inventing" myself, going back to school, starting a new business, etc.
- I've lived all my life being told to expect just this, and this is what I saw with my parents and grandparents and what I'm seeing among all my contemporaries, and so all my plans (and in particular, the money I have set aside) are appropriate for someone who is withdrawing from the world ("retiring").

But if I'm 65 and it's 2007 and I have (or believe I have) two, three, maybe *four* or *five* decades of life remaining, then the attitudes and behaviors change dramatically (even without allowing for the extra dimension of ego that I as a Boomer may bring to the party):

- Objectively, I'm not "old." I have lived only two-thirds of my life, maybe less — maybe I'm only half-way along.
- Therefore, I neither want nor need to think and act "old." However, because I'm objectively not "young," either, I have to find some new "state" — not young, not old. (Thus, the multiple all-ages-in-one Zoomer that Moses Znaimer describes.) I certainly have enough time left to make, and carry out, dramatic new plans. In fact, not to do so would inflict heavy psychological and financial damage. Psychologically, it's unthinkable to withdraw from the world ("retire") for what could be *half a century*. And financially, I can't afford to stop working because I certainly haven't saved up enough money to pay for all those years ahead, especially with everything that's on my plate.
- I may have lived all my life *wanting* this — but it runs counter to everything I have been told to expect, up until very recently. I grew up watching all the previous generations "retire." I watched TV commercials that promoted retirement savings and getting ready for "the golden years" — true, they were aimed at my father's generation, but they did represent the prevailing wisdom. And even today, most government programs use language and imagery that suggests the politicians and bureaucrats imagine me being the same as my parents. Merchants offer me Senior Citizen discount cards! There's a huge disconnect here — I am going to have to break new ground, again.

The contrast between the two sets of circumstances, and the attitudes and behaviors that flow inevitably from those different circumstances, couldn't be clearer.

And that's for people who are 65.

But the oldest Boomers are only 62 — most are still in their 50s. So the shift will be even more dramatic.

I've spent some time on this issue of life expectancy because it provides the all-important *concrete* framework for BoomerAging. The Boomers couldn't create, or sustain, the process through ego, or hubris, or self-absorption alone. If life expectancy were still 65 or 75, the Boomers would be pathetic posturers. It is precisely because life expectancy *is* increasing so dramatically — and maybe even to the point of imminent quantum leaps — that the Boomers are able to provide the rest of the package. Those extra 25, 35, maybe even 50 years — maybe longer — provide the tangible arena in which the BoomerAging production can be mounted. So in examining all the other aspects of BoomerAging, it is important to remember that they are all grounded in the reality of longer . . . much, much longer . . . life spans.

And oh, what the Boomers are doing with it!

CHAPTER 4　**Why is this man smiling?**

Take a look at this guy . . .

Doesn't he seem to epitomize the Boomer we've been talking about? In his 50s, most likely — but youthful-looking, exactly as you'd expect in someone who thinks he's 10–15 years younger than his chronological age. The big wide grin, the demeanor of vigor, of action — he could have stepped out of one of those stockbroker commercials where they show you people without a care in the world, owing it all to the wonderful advice they got from the experts at Insert-Name-of-Investment-Company-Here.

Except for a few things.

First of all, he's still caring for his 80-something mother. He has to pay some of her bills, and there's also a lot of things to worry about: is she sticking to her meds, what if she falls, are the bills being paid . . . it's not a short list. Mom calls him often, and sometimes he has to drop what he's doing and get over there to help her through a crisis, real or imagined. Not that he isn't getting plenty of free advice — from his sister, who lives at the other end of the country and is a forceful armchair critic.

Being a caregiver changes the picture somewhat, doesn't it?

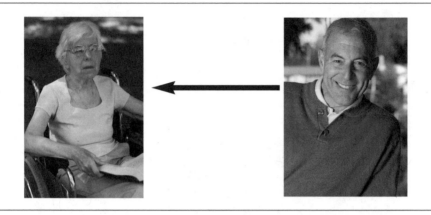

But that's not all.

One of the debates he's having with his sister is about where to put Mom. Sis has a great idea: sell Mom's house and have her move in with — you guessed it — our hero. But even assuming our man could sell this idea to his 15-years-younger Trophy Second Wife (and that's a whole other story), there's still a problem.

The bedroom that would logically be earmarked for Mom is currently occupied. And the occupant is our man's 28-year-old Slacker Son. Still living with his parents and showing no signs of being ready to move out. In fact, there's an on-again, off-again girlfriend whose stuff is in the closet, too.

So now the picture looks like this:

But he's *still* not done.

He has a 26-year-old daughter, who's married and has a home of her own (thank God at least one child has moved out). But she can't afford the daycare fees for her toddler, and our man is absolutely not going to have his beautiful little granddaughter go without *anything*. Not if he can help it. So he's writing the checks for the daycare fees, and the picture now looks like this:

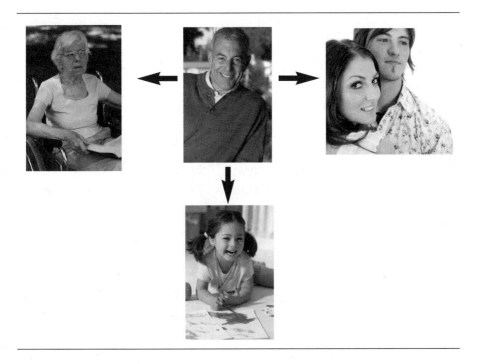

You'd think I'd be ready to show him some mercy, but we're *still* not done.

With all these checks he's writing, and the fact that he didn't really put away enough money in the first place, our man is seriously underfunded. There's no way he can afford to retire, even if he wanted to. It's a terrible thing to say, but he is really going to *need* that two million or so that's in Mom's will — that's *if* it's still all there, depending on how long Mom lives, after the long-term care costs are paid for.

You may think I've loaded this poor fellow up with too many problems and pressures, that I've stacked the deck to create an example that isn't really typical. But our man is the archetype of the so-called Sandwich

Generation — simultaneously taking care of his parents and his children and gradually morphing into the "Club Sandwich" generation, providing help to his grandchildren, too. Let's have a quick look at some of the underlying facts and figures.

1. Caregiving

Most studies show that one in four adults are caregivers, providing about 15 hours a week or more of help to chronically ill or disabled loved ones. This would mean that out of our 100 million or so Boomers in the USA, Canada and Britain, 25 million are caregivers.

Those living in Canada and the UK report a high level of stress as they try to juggle all their responsibilities. A 2001 survey by Statistics Canada found that 66% of "sandwich generation" caregivers reported themselves to be "very" or "somewhat" stressed — and that's if they were providing a "low" level of care to an elderly parent. If the level of care was "high," the percentage who were stressed rose to 76%.

An article in the *Sunday Herald* in December, 2002, reported on a study by the British Social Attitudes Survey, revealing that "sandwich generation" caregivers were "stressed out by family ties, torn between the responsibilities of looking after aging parents and the demands of their children — and by hours spent looking after young grandchildren." The article quoted Rhian Beynon, of the Age Concern research organization: "There is a group caught in the middle who are giving support to their parents and their children. We have seen in our own research that as people are living longer and having families in later life there is a trend towards having to try and reach a balance between these demands, which can be very difficult."

In the USA, the picture is the same — at least, as to the prevalence of "sandwich generation" households. But according to a 2001 study by AARP, American Boomers, unlike their British counterparts, seem to be relatively confident about their ability to handle their many responsibilities.

The study focused on the 45–55 age group — the older Baby Boomers, born between 1946 and 1956 — and found that 54% of them were caring for children, parents or both. But attitudinally, "this generation may be squeezed, but it is not very stressed. Overall, our results describe a generation that is comfortable with and confident of its capacity to manage its family roles. Members of this generation welcome involvement in the care of their loved ones, but are cool to the thought of imposing their own future needs on their children." The AARP notes, in the introduction to the report, "The survey results surprised us. We began the effort thinking that older Baby Boomers would feel enormously burdened by the dual demands of parenting and elder care. Yet the survey analysis sketches a different profile of these boomers — less stressed, more self-assured, and more at ease in their roles than not."

How come? "The generation's demographics may provide some clues. The sandwich generation is generally more likely to be married, better educated and more affluent than the nation as a whole."

Maybe that's why our man is grinning so confidently. He can handle it — or thinks he can. But, as we're seeing, there's a lot to handle.

2. Children still living at home

"They're the 'boomerang' or 'back-to-the-bedroom' kids," writes Jim Hopkins in *USA Today* (January 11, 2005). "They leave. They come back. Sometimes more than once, often after college, between jobs, before marriage, after a divorce or when housing costs are so exorbitant that moving in to their old bedrooms is more appealing than sharing a small, rundown apartment with three roommates."

In Canada, 44% of people aged 20–29 are still living at home with their parents. In the UK, it's so prevalent that the BBC reported (July 18, 2007): "Fed up with their offspring still at home in their twenties, parents are stumping up thousands of pounds to encourage them to move out. Research for the Skipton Building Society showed that parents were prepared to pay an average of £8,000 to help them flee the nest."

3. Financial support for grandchildren

And now throw grandchildren into the mix.

An AARP study found that 21% of grandparents had given "a significant amount" to help pay college tuition fees for their grandchildren, while 22% had provided money for basic needs and 20% provided daycare "on a regular basis" so the parents could work.

UK figures are similar. According to a paper presented in 2007 to a conference sponsored by the Oxford Institute of Aging, 20% of grandparents provide financial support to grandchildren.

Canadian statisticians have been tracking an even more dramatic trend: grandparents actually *raising* the grandchildren, absent the parents. Between 1991 and 2001, the number of children under the age of 18 living *only* with their grandparents in Canada jumped by 20% — and in the USA, by 44%.

4. Underfunded retirement

As we see, a lot of money is going out — but is it coming in?

Experts generally agree that the Boomers are underfunded as far as conventional "retirement" is concerned:

- According to the International Longevity Center in the USA (www.ilcusa.org), "Baby Boomers are not ready for later life." The average Boomer has saved only $100,000 for retirement, and for all the talk about the trillions of dollars the Boomers will inherit as their aging-but-still-alive parents die off, the average Boomer will receive only $47,000 in inheritance. In the 2001 Study of Consumer Finances by the Federal Reserve, it was found that half of all households headed by older Boomers (born between 1945 and 1956) had total financial assets of less than $46,000.

- In Canada, according to a 2006 study conducted by BMO Financial Group, 70% of Baby Boomers said they didn't feel on track with saving for retirement or *didn't even know* if they were on track. But 83% said they were prepared to work longer if they had to. (We'll have a lot more to say on this very important topic in a later chapter.)

- In the UK, a 2006 study carried out by Heyday, a new organization for Boomers and seniors, reported that over 40% of people in their 50s were not yet actively planning for their retirement at all. Almost a quarter of those surveyed said they did not have adequate pensions or savings.

So what does it all add up to?

A very full plate — and the need to keep a large flow of money coming in. This need, this complex menu of responsibilities, anchors the Boomer-Aging process in the concrete, makes it much more than just Boomer ego at play. The notion of "retirement" — removal from activity — is quite simply impossible, let alone culturally or emotionally desirable.

So why is this man smiling?

Because he believes he can handle it. He *wants* to handle it — indeed, the entire ethos to which he subscribes tells him he *has* to handle it.

But there are other places those checks are going, too. Other things happening in his life that contribute — significantly — to that smile.

Let's take a look at some of them.

CHAPTER 5 The SKIers

Unlike their parents and grandparents, Boomers show no inclination to worry about leaving much money behind. Not when there's so much to spend it on today.

Not surprisingly, they're very unapologetic about it. There's even an acronym — SKIing — Spending the Kids' Inheritance. And of course, if you're going to be a SKIer, you might as well glory in it.

You can buy SKIing licence plate covers . . .

I'M SPENDING MY KIDS' INHERITANCE

. . . and bumper stickers . . .

Spending the kids' inheritance!

. . . on eBay. Apparently they're quite popular on RVs and luxury cars — the aging Boomers want to make it quite plain there's absolutely no guilt attached to splurging.

As you might expect, there's a burgeoning industry in SKIing advice. Some of it purports to be serious, like this book published in the UK in 2006 by *Coronation Street* star Annie Hulley.

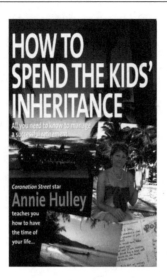

Hulley, who made a fortune in real estate and authored *How to Be A Property Millionaire*, takes a serious approach to the topic, arguing that SKIing is an outright necessity:

> Our Edwardian ancestors did not enjoy the longevity that we do and it
> is becoming clear that a life of 'toil today with the hope of rest to-
> morrow' is no longer practical. An aging population puts a burden on
> society as a whole, particularly the young, and it seems unlikely that
> the offspring of the 'SKI' generation will be able to enjoy the same
> 'golden age' as their parents did. Everyone is living longer so you might
> have to 'Spend The Kids' Inheritance' (SKI) in order to survive.

At the other extreme is this effort by Tad and Alicia Carrier Box-
mueller, glorying in the utter irresponsibility of it all. Now you're not just
spending the kids' inheritance, you're "blowing your bank wad" altogether.
The sub-head is particularly vivid: "More Than 101 Scandalous Ways to
Squander Your Kids' Inheritance." *Squander*, if you please.

The book may be tongue-in-cheek, but there's nothing comical about
the trend. An article in the *Daily Telegraph* in September of 2005 cited a
survey by the Joseph Rowntree Foundation, indicating that two in three UK

adults with the means to make a bequest said they planned "to enjoy life and not worry too much about leaving a legacy." Here we see the Boomer ethos already trickling down to younger generations (and come to think of it, take a look at the couple on the cover of *Blow Your Bank Wad* . . . and the age of the kids standing helplessly on the porch).

The SKIing acronym is also widely used in Australia, as per this 2003 article on Australia's ABC.net, reporting on the Commonwealth Bank's introduction of reverse mortgages. The acronym becomes a bit more urgent with the addition of N for *Now*:

> It's a standing joke among many Australian retirees, many of whom only half-seriously refer to 'Spending the Kids' Inheritance Now.' But possibly picking up on a shift in social values, Australia's biggest home lender, the Commonwealth Bank, is about to make it a lot easier to do. The so-called reverse mortgage is already offered by St. George Bank. But the Commonwealth will . . . become the first of the big four to offer a product that effectively means that customers can 'spend their homes' in retirement and settle their account from the grave.

I particularly love "settle their account from the grave."

As always, a good indicator of the strength of the SKIing idea can quickly be found with a Google search. I punched in "Spending the kids' inheritance" and instantly got about 690,000 results:

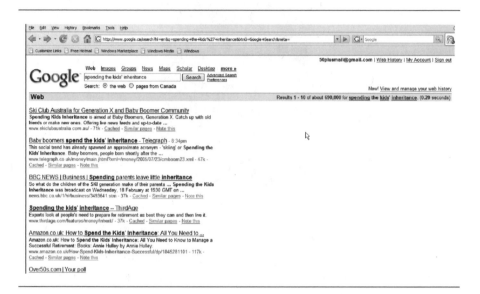

From serious to frivolous, from life-or-death ("I absolutely need the money") to discretionary ("I could be leaving it in my will but — ha-ha-ha — I'm not"), the Boomers — and in particular, the wealthier ones (per Moses Znaimer, the Zoomers) — are spending enough money on enough things that they're far and away the most important segment of the marketplace.

In a later chapter, we'll break that spending down — and show how woefully slowly the media/marketing/advertising industry has caught on. What matters at this point is to nail down the psychology, the attitude, because that's what bears most directly on BoomerAging.

A book released in May 2007 highlighted the important differences in attitude between the Baby Boomers and their parents. The book, *Baby Boomers and Their Parents: Surprising Findings on Their Lifestyles, Mindsets and Well-Being*, was co-authored by Professor Anil Mathir of Hofstra University and Professor George Moschis of Georgia State University.

When it came to money, they found, Boomers were much more ready to indulge themselves now than to worry about the future:

- Boomers were more concerned than their parents about maintaining their current standards of living as they aged; their parents were relatively more ready to downsize, cut back, etc. in response to living on a fixed income.
- Boomers said they had a harder time than their parents in keeping up with the weekly bills.
- Boomers said they had a harder time than their parents in paying off credit cards.
- Boomers were much more concerned with being able to keep on working, or to go back to work, in some form, after "retirement."
- Boomers were much more concerned than their parents with being able to spec out the details of a satisfactory retirement.

It's not hard to understand where these differences come from. The Boomers' parents — the 'Greatest Generation' — lived through the Great Depression and World War II. The experiences made them cautious savers, relatively more likely to be pessimistic about the future (or at least not have stars in their eyes), relatively more likely to accept their lot (because experience had shown them it could always be worse). Their childhoods were shaped by cataclysmic *deflation* when cash was king.

The Boomers, by contrast, grew up being taught that all things were possible, and all things could be theirs — an attitude which, as we are seeing, remains with them. They also grew up in an era of *inflation*, when borrowing was not only culturally or emotionally satisfying (because it produced instant gratification), but also a very rational strategy in cold-blooded financial terms: borrow all you can because you're paying off in inflated dollars. The Boomers have always been whipsawed by two kinds of forces: emotional/attitudinal ("The default position is 'Me, me, me'") and concrete ("You see? There's hard evidence that 'Me, me, me' is correct"). Money is no exception. The oldest Boomers were on their second house, and starting to earn those corner offices, when Jimmy Carter was president. The prime rate touched 21.5% in December 1980. Who but an idiot would be *saving* money under such circumstances?

And besides, there were all those toys to keep buying...

And so we arrive at where we are today.

American mutual fund giant Fidelity Investments reported on the sorry state of retirement savings in 2005. Noting that most experts recommend that people have enough savings to generate 85% of pre-retirement income, the report showed how far off that target the savings actually were:

- Americans born in 1950 or earlier either had, or were on track to accumulate, enough savings to generate only 62% of pre-retirement incomes.
- Americans born between 1951 and 1964 were in the same boat — enough savings to generate 63% of pre-retirement incomes.
- And, proving my theory that the Boomer influence is percolating down to the generations coming in behind them, Americans born later than 1965 were on track to accumulate enough savings to generate only 55% of pre-retirement incomes, or only two-thirds of what they were going to need.

The picture isn't much different in Canada. A 2006 report by Statistics Canada shows clearly the decline in savings rates today, compared to only 20 years ago:

Savings by married couples	Age 55 to 64		Age 65 to 74		Age 75+	
Year of survey	1982	2003	1982	2003	1982	2003
Year(s) born	1918–1927	1939–1949	1908–1917	1929 1938	1907 and earlier	1928 and earlier
% of income disbursed on "savings"	16	3	13	4	22	10

Table 4 — % of income disbursed as "savings," married couples, 1982 vs. 2003

Twenty-five years ago, Canadians in the pre-retirement (55–64) age group put 16% of their income into savings; in 2003, it was just 3%. People in the first tranche of post-retirement (65–74) put 13% of their income into savings; in 2003, only 4%. The oldest group (75+) put 22% — almost a quarter — of their income into savings; in 2003, only 10%.

In the UK, according to a 2006 survey by Hartford Financial Services Group, 70% of workers over the age of 45 worry that they won't have enough savings for retirement, and 25% believe they won't live as well as their parents. (Similar figures were generated from US workers.)

As with all the other trends we're studying, it's the *combination* that does the damage, that makes BoomerAging so inexorable. If it were just attitudes — there go the Boomers spreading that money around — you could argue that the effects might be transitory, that a future generation might revert to the penny-pinching "oldness" of the Boomers' own parents. But take the Boomers' life-long predilection to spend (and, what's more, to *borrow* in order to spend), and add in all the concrete forces that make the spending necessary, and you have an irresistible outcome: SKIing. And SKIing, in turn, is just another dimension of BoomerAging: if you're spending, you're active, you're engaged; if you're saving, you're more likely to be removed from the action, "retired."

As this schematic shows, it's hardly an equal contest.

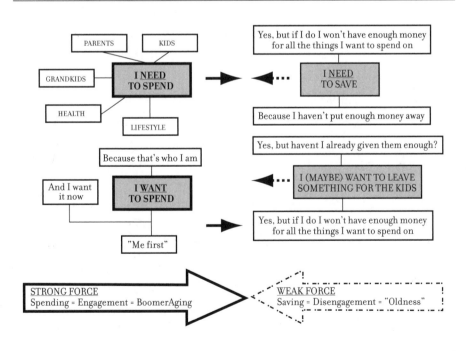

Fig. 8 — How need and attitude combine to create SKIing

It's important to understand that the Boomers are *not* unaware of the shortfall in so-called "retirement" savings. As we'll see in a later chapter, a big part of their solution is simply to keep on working. Nothing — and certainly not the traditional views of "retirement" — can be permitted to slow down the check writing. If there's not enough money in the nest egg, then keep on getting more. If that revolutionizes the concept of retirement, if it puts a roadblock in the path of upward mobility for the generation coming in behind, too bad.

Note, too, how many Boomers realize that their spending needs and wants may wind up producing — when they eventually do stop working — "retirement years" that may not be as comfortable as what their parents enjoyed. What's significant here is that this recognition is *not* driving them to change their habits in the here and now, cut back spending, introduce austerity programs, etc. They see it all coming; they're confident they can stickhandle around it; they're aware that if they fail in that stickhandling effort they may wind up worse off than their own parents at the same age . . .

And the spending continues.

In fact, as we've seen, they make light of it. "I'm SKIing," they boast. "I'm spending the kids' inheritance." Thus they turn what may be a financially ruinous program into a culturally hip activity. But why not? This is exactly what they did with other potentially ruinous activities when they were younger, gliding smoothly (and at times not so smoothly) from hippiedom to the conspicuous consumption of yuppiehood.

As Moses Znaimer said, describing this generation, "It's about 'me'; it's always been about 'me.'"

Yes. For sure. But that doesn't mean it's all frivolous. Remember those "sandwich generation" responsibilities — they *are*, it must be noted, being met. And it should also be noted that a key part what has been called the "Die Broke" philosophy (there was a best-selling book with that title) includes being generous with your children while you are still alive, so that both you and they could appreciate the process. "Die Broke" meant you were shafting the *undertaker* . . . not necessarily your own children.

If it sounds like I'm hedging a few bets here, or presenting a slightly ambiguous picture, that's exactly what I am doing. Because, as with so much that goes on as Boomers develop and perfect BoomerAging, there is always a mixture of factors in play. Point, counterpoint. A relentless determination to meet the multi-generational responsibilities, to juggle so many balls at once, to keep on working as long and as hard as it takes. Yet, at the same time, a devil-may-care denial of ticking time bombs — and a stubborn refusal to compromise on profligate financial habits. And then, for style points, the conscious decision to laugh at it all, to wrap it up with a little black humor: SKIing.

How perfect. How like the Boomers to be absolutely unapologetic, un-embarrassed. The Boomers have always had a certain twinkle in the eye about themselves and what they do, a streak of the rascal, a sense of getting away with something.

Dylan Thomas, who died when the oldest Boomers were eight years old, urged a harsh and angry resistance to aging. In his mind, "old age should rage and burn at close of day" — *that* was the method by which you "did not go gentle into that good night."

The Boomers agree as to the objective — they're certainly not "going gentle into that good night" — but not the technique. Not for them the futile energy of "raging and burning." Instead, they "de-age": first re-defining the whole thing, then re-engineering as many of the components as they can, all the while laughing at their own insouciance and, when push finally comes to shove and they face the prospect of the money running out . . . well, who has to think about *that* just yet?

It was not for nothing that one of the cultural icons of the older Boomers' childhood — Alfred E. Neuman of *MAD* magazine — had as his motto: "What, me worry?"

So the Boomers just dress it all up as SKIing . . . and keep swiping those credit cards.

CHAPTER 6 **I'm gonna spend forever**

In the last chapter, we established two motives for the Boomers spending the kids' inheritance:

> · "I *want* to spend"
> and
> "I *need* to spend"

In this chapter, we're going to take a closer look at where that spending is going. And I hope it will become clear that it isn't just a question of dollar volume (although the Boomers do dominate the market). More than that: the *qualitative* nature of that spending is, in itself, a key aspect of Boomer-Aging. The Boomers are spending precisely in order to stay young, to *remain engaged* — in some cases, to pioneer.

In previous generations, spending became more conservative with aging. "Retirement," don't forget, meant disengaging, withdrawing from active life. It also usually meant living on a fixed income, and even where that income was more than adequate (which was the whole point of the classic model of "putting money away for your retirement"), absolute dollar spending tended to decrease. There was little or no appetite for fashion, there was no point in thinking about trying to stay young or beautiful, travel tended to be restricted to tried-and-true locations relatively close to home, and while worn-out appliances or furniture might certainly be replaced by newer models, there was little desire to engage with new technology. Housing was largely a matter of downsizing, or abandoning the category altogether (often out of necessity) in favor of institutionalized care.

In previous generations, attitude fed reality fed attitude in a continuous loop. The schematic on the next page illustrates the self-reinforcing effects of attitudes and actions on the part of "seniors" and on the part of the marketplace.

As we will see, BoomerAging is destroying every single one of those patterns of thought and action.

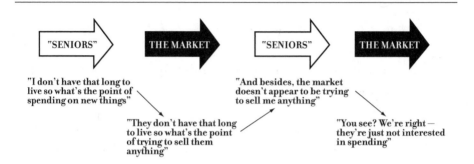

Fig. 9 — "Seniors Don't Spend" — the self-reinforcing cycle of attitudes and actions that has applied throughout history . . . until BoomerAging

The big categories of Boomer spending — surprise, surprise — all relate to themselves and their immediate environment:

- Health — as a simple practical matter of trying to live longer and more comfortably
- "Wellness" and beauty — in order to actualize that vision of themselves as 10–15 years younger than their chronological age
- Technology — for three main reasons: (a) the pure enjoyment of the products, (b) to enable them to keep working, and (c) to mitigate the effects of aging
- Travel and leisure — because the Boomers see no reason to stop pursuing pleasurable experiences
- Housing — because the Boomers are determined never to end up in a nursing home

While the specifics of what the Boomers are buying, and how much they are spending, varies from category to category, there is a common set of attitudes and approaches that governs the entire shopping and spending

process. It is here — well before we start looking at actual products or services — that we can identify the first important influences of BoomerAging.

1. Brand loyalty is dead

Numerous research studies have shown Boomers are no more brand loyal
than younger consumers, and significantly *less* brand loyal than previous
generations of the same age.

Chuck Underwood, founder of consultancy The Generational Imperative, commented in a 2003 article in the *Cincinnati Business Courier*,
"What's happening? Two phenomena. First, boomers possess astonishing
purchasing power and they spend their money freely; they are, after all, the
instant-gratification generation. Second, and this is the big one, boomers
are the first generation that will go through their entire lives with absolutely
no brand loyalty.

"Boomers are famous for wanting to make the smartest possible
buying decision every single time. That means they insist on being open to
new products and services and to changing brands the moment another
brand offers superior quality and value."

Mike Irwin, president of Focalyst Research, echoed this theme in a
2006 presentation of the findings of an extensive brand loyalty survey
carried out by his firm, "Marketers who continue to assume that consumer
loyalty and affinity for products and services remains fixed as people age
will lose market share to those who seek out and directly speak to them."

2. Boomers are enthusiastic researchers

"It's time to throw out the notion that the only things marketable to this
market segment are chiropractic mattresses, cruises for older adults, or an
arthritis drug," writes consultant Brent Green in *Marketing to Leading-Edge
Baby Boomers*. "It's a myth that you can't teach an old dog new tricks. On the
contrary, people over 50 are some of the heaviest users of the Internet for
research and product buying."

This is hardly surprising. The Boomers, remember, were the yuppies
of the late 1970s, arguably the most intense shoppers of all time. They've
always known how to keep track of the latest and greatest — why should now
be any different?

With the advent of the Internet, it's easier by orders of magnitude to check out what's new, and to compare prices. And here's an instance where the Insanely Active Shopper influence of BoomerAging is trickling *upward*, and affecting the habits of those in their 70s and even older.

A couple of chapters ago, I mentioned a focus group we'd recently conducted at ZoomerMedia — the one where people said "old" meant 87 and that they hated being called "seniors." The age range in the group was 60 to 73.

Before the formal group discussion got underway, the folks were taking their seats, pouring a coffee, introducing themselves. We watched, fascinated, from our side of the glass.

"I found Vero Beach for under $200 one-way on Expedia yesterday," one woman volunteered. She was 68.

"Expedia? I never have good luck there," said a 67-year-old man. "I like Travelocity better. Just last week, I found Fort Lauderdale for $120 one-way."

"You're kidding," the woman said. "Let me write that down."

And they went on for another 15 minutes, comparing travel discount websites, before the moderator was finally able to bring them to order.

3. Boomers see themselves as taking more risks and being more adventurous — not less — as they get older

This point was made very explicitly in a 2006 study of 1,500 Boomers by the Natural Marketing Institute, who found that *half* the Boomers surveyed considered themselves risk-takers and felt more adventurous as they grew older. (The study also found that six out of ten considered themselves spenders rather than savers.)

And, according to the survey by American Express Financial Advisors, 85% of Boomers view their so-called "retirement" as a time for "learning and self-discovery," 65% for "re-inventing oneself" and 51% for a "new beginning."

The theme here is obvious: *proactive pursuit*, not passive withdrawal. BoomerAging relentlessly seeks out the cash register for what is new, what is different.

With these underlying attitudes in mind, let's now survey what is actually being purchased in the big categories. This is not intended to be an exhaustive statistical survey of the marketplace; I'm deliberately going to be zeroing in on some of the leading-edge trends, the more interesting patterns that demonstrate how Boomer spending illustrates and reinforces BoomerAging.

As you read through this next section, try to juxtapose "oldness" with what the Boomers are doing now. Here's a reminder:

   *Isaac Kravitz   Sarah Lappin*

My two archetypes of "oldness" again. Try to imagine them going into the marketplace and behaving like what you're about to read. I think it will be very clear how Boomer spending is, in and of itself, an act of destroying and then replacing the traditional concepts of aging.

Health

This is the most intuitively obvious category. As the body ages, even healthy people will encounter more chronic conditions and will need to spend more money on health. The 2003 Consumer Expenditure Survey in the USA broke down the percentage of health spending by age group. Here are the figures:

Age	% of health spending
Under 25	2
25–35	10
36–44	18
45–54	21
55–64	18
65+	31

Table 5 — Spending on health care by age, USA, per 2003 Consumer Expenditure Survey

The age breaks in the table don't precisely line up with Boomer ages (that year, the oldest Boomer was 58 and the youngest was just turning 40), but we can calculate that the Boomers accounted for well over 50% of the spending.

A similar pattern applies in Canada, where Boomers account for over 50% of spending in pharmacies (and the Zoomers — Boomers plus the rest of 50+ population —account for over 80% of that spending).

Boomers both want to and *need to* spend a lot of money on health. Staying healthy is obviously a key part of BoomerAging — it's simply impossible to do all that they want to do if they're infirm. At the same time, publicly funded health care is unable to cope with aging of the population, and Boomers are in no mood to wait in a queue while the government figures it all out. There are powerful new therapies, products and services that can promote longevity and better health, and Boomers will do what they have to do to acquire them.

Take something as simple as exercise.

The traditional image of the health club was as a place for young people — all those lean, hard bodies running on the treadmills and lifting the weights. No place for oldies, no place for fatties because, if nothing else, it could be embarrassing to display your relative lack of fitness and form.

Not any more. By 2000, according to a survey reported in *American Fitness*, Boomers had become the largest single age group in health clubs, accounting for 38% of members (compared to Gen Xers at 36%). The clubs themselves have responded, some better than others, by trying to create a less intimidating environment. There has also been a dramatic growth in the use of personal trainers, which plays neatly into the Boomers' desire for high levels of service. One major franchise, Fitness Together, has built its entire business on offering every client a personal trainer.

The next logical step is a fitness club catering *only* to Boomers, and there are already promising signs. When our flagship site, 50plus.com, carried an article about an entrepreneur who started such a club, we not only generated a huge volume of clicks, but the article produced a flood of requests for the club to expand into other cities.

Here was the original article . . .

Fitness, boomer-style

Article By: Cynthia Ross Cravit

Disappointed by youth-oriented health clubs, Cleo Chmielinski creates her own...and business is booming.

During a routine check-up with her doctor, Cleo Chmielinski received advice that may sound familiar: find a way to incorporate more exercise into your life.

After years of finding excuses not to exercise, Cleo finally took this advice to heart and started searching for a health club. But she was turned off by the entire scene. "I didn't feel very comfortable with all the 20-somethings in spandex," says Cleo, who is a 40-something baby boomer. "Even worse, I found the trainers generally weren't interested in my needs. They seemed more interested in the younger members."

And from that experience, the idea for Avalon Woods – a health club geared toward mature adults – was born. "I thought to myself: there must be people like me, searching for a health club more suited for mature needs and tastes," Cleo says of her decision to open the club.

. . . and some of the reader comments that were posted on the site:

I am currently a member of Goodlife, but would certainly feel more comfortable at a club like this. I know people would join a club if it catered to over 50s, come to Chatham, Ont. — Linda

I would really love to see a club like this in Calgary, Alberta. Would there be any chance of this happening? — Barbara

What a unique concept. I like the idea that a gym is geared to my age and strengths. As Joan stated, when are you coming West?? I have RA, this causes me to very careful on what or what not I can do at a gym. — Jay

Hello. Wow! Good for you. I have quit exercising clubs because of the very same reasons. I am in Burlington. If you ever expand here let me know. You could start off with a small shop. There are sooooooo many seniors here. I know they would be interested. — Aprile

Hi, I am 68 and have osteoarthritis but love to exercise. I need to know what I can do safely without making my joints any worse. If your club comes to central Toronto, will it meet my needs? — M. Schulz

But exercise and health clubs, while representing a huge dollar volume of spending, are just the tip of the iceberg. More revolutionary will be the spending on high tech health, including replacement body parts. Already some of these are being marketed directly to consumers.

Can you *brand* a knee? A *shoulder*?

Here's the home page for Biomet Inc., which manufactures products for hip, knee, shoulder, elbow and small joint replacement.

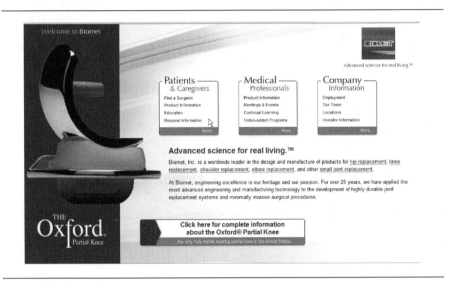

The Oxford Partial Knee is the featured product, but there are plenty more. Other Biomet knee systems include Vanguard, the Ascent Total Knee System, the Maxim Complete Knee System. Among other products, there are also the BioModular Shoulder System, the Mosaic Humeral Replacement System, the Integral 180 Hip System, and the Progressive Total Hip System.

What's interesting is that these are being marketed, at least in part, directly to consumers. As you can see from the home page menu, there is an entire section of the website devoted to "Patients and Caregivers," and it features content that is typical of marketing in other consumer categories. For example, there are celebrity endorsers, like gymnastics gold medalist

Mary Lou Retton and former University of Wisconsin football coach Barry Alvarez, who deliver video testimonials about how their lives were changed by one of the BioMet systems.

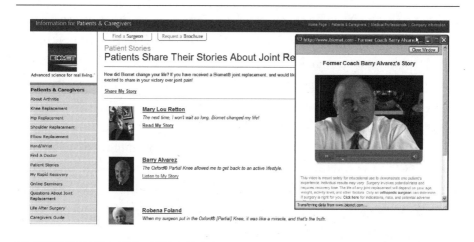

And in case you're worried that the procedure may be too painful or that the recovery may be too complicated or prolonged, there's another whole section of the website dedicated to reassuring you.

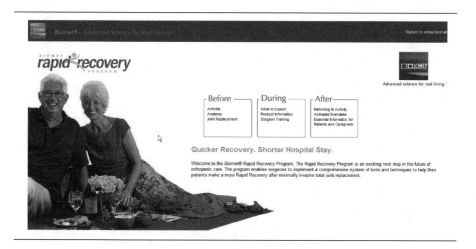

Now it's obvious that you can't just go out and *buy* one of these systems. Your doctor's opinion — and referral — is going to be decisive. But I think it's significant that the company believes it's important to influence *your*

opinion, as well. Clearly, they recognize that the patient is becoming a major factor in health care decision-making today.

The BioMet example confirms what I said about how BoomerAging differs from previous generations when it comes to health. "Oldness" — as characterized by Isaac Kravitz and Sarah Lappin — meant taking an essentially passive approach to health. If you weren't sick, you didn't go to the doctor. When you got sick, you went — and whatever he told you, it was gospel. The idea that you could be a *player* in the process was unthinkable. The idea that the manufacturers of drugs or products would bother to talk to *you*, the mere patient, was ridiculous.

In case you think the BioMet site is an isolated example, we can quickly validate what's happening with a Google search. I typed in "Compare knee replacements" and got nearly *two million results*, including websites that compare products and services, websites that offer free quotes, and even websites that compare other websites.

Notice some of the paid aids on the right:

- "High quality knee surgery abroad at very low prices"
- "Find knee replacement options"
- "The amazing Oxford or CustomFit total replacement"
- "Stop searching. We have the top 5 sites for knee replacement surgery"

Now Oxford, as we just learned, is one of the BioMet brands. So here we have a *dealer* who will actually perform the surgery, promoting the brand name product we will be using. Did I say *dealer*? He's an MD! But in the new world of patient-driven health care, with a huge audience of empowered Boomers behaving just like shoppers, the doctor (admittedly not in all environments) might be morphing into just another form of retailer.

Okay, but joint replacement — vital as it may be if you're suffering — is surely not in the same category as life-or-death medical treatment. There's no way the patient could be as involved in, say . . . cardiac surgery.

Right?

Wrong.

I went back to Google and typed in something that I honestly thought would be improbable: "Discount heart surgery."

Once again, almost *two million results*. And even allowing for the imprecision of the search and the irrelevancy of many of the items, the net outcome is startling.

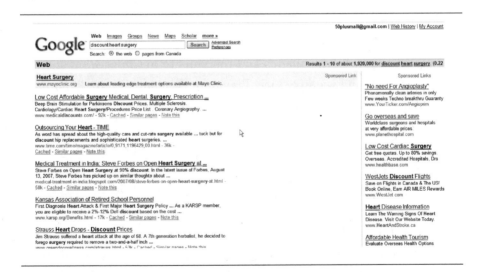

Again, look at some of the paid ads on the right:

- "Go overseas and save"
- "Low cost cardiac surgery"

- "Affordable health tourism" (Yes, health and tourism combined; we'll have more to say about this in the next few pages)
- "No need for angioplasty. Phenomenally clean arteries in few weeks. Techno breakthrough."

It's obvious, because of the nature of the categories themselves — joint replacement, cardiac surgery — that these messages are aimed at Boomers. Clearly, the providers of these products and services have figured out that the Boomers are proactive, have the dollars and will do what they perceive is necessary to buy better health.

The Boomers are transforming health care by turning *patients* into *shoppers*. Thanks to BoomerAging, the doctor — even the hospital — becomes, in the end, just another store. It may only be a matter of time before BioMet offers 0% financing, or end-of-season clearances.

"Wellness" and beauty

This category is closely related to health, and the impact of BoomerAging is just as big. It's also one of the few categories in which marketers have finally realized how important the Boomers are.

"It's not about turning back the clock. It is about getting her the formula, the system, the shades and the tools to optimize what she has today," said Revlon Executive Vice-President Stephanie Klein-Peponis in a 2006 interview on MSNBC.com, talking about the launch of Revlon's new Vital Radiance line. Revlon used actress Susan Sarandon as the celebrity endorser. "Susan Sarandon is perfect for the Revlon brand," Klein-Peponis went on to say. "Her beauty and talent have broad appeal. We are thrilled to be working with her."

Susan Sarandon was 58 when the product launched.

Diane Keaton was even older — 60 — when L'Oréal Paris signed her as spokesperson for its new Age Perfect skin products. Carol Hamilton, president of L'Oréal Paris, said, "Diane has been a role model and a trendsetter for over three decades, and we feel that she is the perfect example to show that women can be beautiful, full of vitality and incredibly successful in every stage of their lives." Could there be a better précis of BoomerAging?

Dove, however, pushed the idea even further: instead of anti-aging, it took a stand for *pro*-aging and for the idea that you can be beautiful at any age. The campaign features real women — not Photoshopped models. Dove says on its website, "We created pro-age™ products and invited women in their best years to show the world that beauty has no age limit by appearing in our next ad. Thousands embraced the pro-age™ challenge answered our casting call to be the next Dove real women."

Dove pushed the idea of ageless beauty even further by running a series of ads and commercials featuring Boomer (and older) women in the nude — tastefully shot, of course, but nude nonetheless. Here's an example:

The logic of the Dove campaign stands all our traditional concepts of aging on their heads — being beautiful at any age also implies being more engaged at any age.

This doesn't necessarily mean, of course, just "letting yourself go" and calling it "beautiful." While aging Boomers may be happy to have their "beauty quotient" validated — by big-name stars like Diane Keaton or Susan Sarandon, as well as by the "real women" of the Dove campaign — they are also spending a lot of time and money looking for every way possible to look and feel younger than their chronological age.

That's one of the reasons for the explosive growth of medical spas, which combine traditional spa treatments with prescription drugs and medical procedures. Virtually non-existent until about five years ago, the medical spa today represents the hottest segment of the spa industry — the number of medical spas in the USA, for example, jumped 50% between 2005 and 2006.

According to a March 2007 report in Amednews.com, which provides news for physicians, the number is expected to climb a further 33% in 2007. The report quotes Susie Ellis, president of Spa Finder Inc., a spa trend watcher: "The baby boomers are fuelling it."

Already the industry is well-enough developed to be generating sub-categories, or specialty niches. While Boomer women are the main target market, there are now medical spas specializing in men's services, including sexual health counseling, hormone therapy, skin tightening, and vein treatment. There are spas that specialize in age management, offering hormone therapy, diet, nutrition and exercise regimens all designed to combat aging. There are spas based in hospitals, where recovering patients and their families can get better together. There are even dental spas, offering the latest in teeth whitening and dental reconstruction techniques.

Industry watcher Spatrade.com predicted this growth in 2005: "Medical spas will continue to thrive as consumers seek a nurturing/caring environment and more control over their health regimes. Blending traditional medical expertise with spa luxury and innovation, medical spas are becoming trusted venues for executive physicals, health and wellness programs, cosmetic treatments, dentistry and dermatology. Medical spas will also continue to earn the respect of the traditional medical community as mainstream physicians continue to embrace proven alternative therapies, insurers continue to recognize the value of preventative spa therapies, and cosmetic procedures become increasingly valuable annuities for elite doctors." This last point is important — medical spas have become a way for physicians to diversify their incomes. Think I was exaggerating when I said, a few paragraphs ago, that the doctors were morphing into just another kind of store?

This is all driven by BoomerAging — another example of the Boomer as a *consumer* of (real or perceived) health-creating products and services, rather than the passive "I just hope I don't have to go to the doctor" demonstrator of "oldness," as per previous generations.

And, as with everything else the Boomers are seeking, the quickest and most comprehensive reference point is the Internet. "Medical spas" returns over two million results on Google.

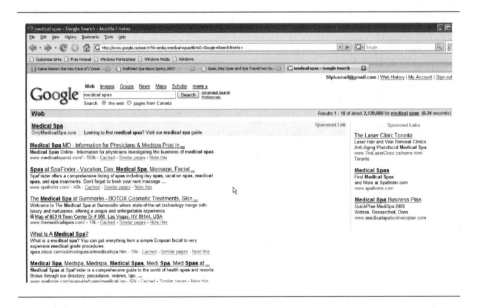

But, as noted above, there are many sub-specialties within this category. "Dental spas" returns almost as many results (see next page).

How does a dental office morph into a *spa*?

A good example is the Atlanta Center for Cosmetic Dentistry, whose website has the intriguing name www.georgiasmiles.com. Here patients can sit in a high-tech "Zen chair" which vibrates as patients listen to soothing

music through earphones. "It puts you into a deep relaxation state," explained Dr. Debra Gray King in a 2003 interview on Foxnews.com. After the dental procedures, the patients can receive a full-body massage from a masseuse.

The website presents the center as if it were a high fashion boutique, complete with celebrity endorsements, a panoramic video tour, and links to many broadcast reports that featured the facility. We learn that Dr. King was one of "the dream team of doctors" working on the ABC hit series *Extreme Makeover*. And Dr. Will Hoskyns is the only cosmetic dentist to perform smile enhancements on the MTV hit *I Want A Famous Face*. Grammy Award–winner Toni Braxton enthuses, "There's not another dental practice like this in Manhattan or Beverly Hills or Atlanta!" If that doesn't impress you, there's Dr. King again, smiling beside Rudy Giuliani, with whom she appeared at a convention in Las Vegas (where else?) on "Leadership in Dentistry."

Not that it's all vague image-building, either. The center obviously recognizes that today's breed of patient demands a lot of information up front, and the site includes a detailed description of what to expect. Not surprisingly, high tech plays a big role. The services include a "smile analysis" and "computerized imaging" of what you could look like afterward. "First we listen to your wants and desires for your smile," the website explains. "Then we take digital and diagnostic photographs necessary to create an image that is designed to closely correspond to your desires to see if you like it. At this time we will discuss your smile analysis, and show you computer-enhanced images of your own features with expertly crafted restorations, natural-looking veneers or crowns. This method allows you to preview possible results using our computer imaging technology and work together to make any changes you'd like." Through technology, apparently, dentistry becomes fashion; shopping for a new face becomes like shopping for a new suit.

In fact, "shopping" is the operative word — and addressed quite frankly on the same page of the website. "If you are price shopping for cosmetic dental care," we are warned, "bear this in mind — just like all restaurants, cars, or hotel rooms are not the same — you would never purchase one because it was the cheapest one you could find — all cosmetic dental offices are not alike. With such a high degree of artistry, technology and science needed for optimal results, there are at least two health care professionals you should not skimp on — your brain surgeon and your cosmetic dentist." Imagine. Skimping on "your" brain surgeon. The idea!

Here are all the components of BoomerAging rolled into one experience — "I want what's new, I want what's hot, I want what's famous, I want what keeps me looking young, I want the latest technology, I want to be pampered, I want, I want . . . " (And I'm willing to pay.)

Do I need to re-insert those photos of Isaac Kravitz and Sarah Lappin at this point, to emphasize how far we've come?

Travel and leisure

It's not exactly dramatic news to observe that Boomers (as well as those who are older) dominate the travel market. They have the time and they have the money (or enough of them have the money) to make up, collectively, by far the largest market segment. According to a recent AARP study, for example, Americans Boomers in 2004 accounted for 44% of all travel spending.

But BoomerAging, as we've seen, is more than just how many dollars are spent — it's *how* those dollars are spent. And when it comes to travel, the Boomers are emphatically *not* behaving as people of the same age behaved in the past. Not for them the gentle, tried-and-true, safe, boring, and relaxing "rests" in familiar locations. A little sun, a little beach, a little shuffleboard, the Seniors' Buffet at 5:30 in the afternoon, and then nighty-night . . .

Not a chance.

The Boomers want new experiences. If they can, they want physical adventure. If they're not in shape for "extreme" travel, they want adventure of the intellectual or emotional variety. They are constantly seeking out what is different — what will take them to a new place (or to a familiar place, but in a new way) and give them an experience they haven't had before. And as fast as they're doing the seeking, the travel industry is doing the providing.

According to an AARP study (2005), 55% of Boomers consider themselves as adventurous and 77% report that their travel experiences are more adventurous than those of their parents.

Not surprisingly, they reject many of the traditional ways of "packaging" travel for "seniors." They don't like over-programmed group tours, they don't like to be identified with "seniors' discounts," and they resist anything that smacks of "been-there-done-that." Research carried out in the USA by the National Tour Association reported that "the overwhelming perception of tour packages by NTA focus group participants was negative," according to a 2007 article on the Association of Travel Marketing Executives website.

Where *are* they going, then, and what are they doing?

A very good clue can be found on my company's main website, www.50plus.com. Our travel section is one of the biggest and best-read on the site (we track all clicks relentlessly); we also produce a bi-weekly travel e-newsletter, which has over 125,000 opt-in subscribers. Here are a few shots of some of our most popular recent articles:

50Plus.com

Sign-up for our newsletters.

HOME PAGE
HEALTH
MONEY
TRAVEL
TODAY'S FEATURE ARTICLES
   ♦ LIVE LIKE A KING
   ♦ TOP DESTINATIONS FOR WOMEN
   ♦ LA DOLCE VITA
   ♦ THE BUZZ ON BOUTIQUE HOTELS
   ♦ SHARE YOUR TRAVELS
FEATURE TRAVEL LINKS
   ♦ BROWSE ALL ARTICLES
   ♦ CARP TRAVEL
   ♦ TRAVEL DISCOUNTS
   ♦ CAR RENTAL DISCOUNTS
   ♦ TRAVEL CLASSIFIEDS
   ♦ VACATION RENTALS
   ♦ NEWSLETTER
SEARCH TRAVEL TOPICS

Sun, sea and - surgery?

Article By: Cynthia Ross Cravit

Need surgery, will travel. More Canadians, tired of long waiting times for medical procedures, are taking advantage of the exploding health tourism industry.

Need surgery? How about a little adventure safari or a discounted tropical vacation on the side?

Medical tourism – where patients go to another country for urgent or elective medical procedures – has become a worldwide, multibillion-dollar industry. In fact, international travel agents say that it is one of the fastest growing segments of the travel industry, more than doubling last year.

An estimated 90,000 Canadians sought treatment in the United States and abroad last year alone, according to a report in The National Post.

And while medical tourists from Canada often seek treatment abroad because they're frustrated by long waiting times, the idea has worldwide appeal. US citizens are lured by drastic cost-savings for most medical procedures, sometimes paying less than a quarter or even as little as a tenth as what they'd pay at home. Yet other

Medical tourism is one of the fastest-growing categories of travel. Fed up with long wait times or high costs at home, the medical tourist gets the needed treatment faster or cheaper (or both) and builds into the package a little sightseeing in an exotic location. Numerous packagers are working this hot new niche — Google returns over six million results.

Sign-up for our newsletters.

HOME PAGE

HEALTH

MONEY

TRAVEL

TODAY'S FEATURE ARTICLES

- LIVE LIKE A KING
- TOP DESTINATIONS FOR WOMEN
- SUN, SEA AND - SURGERY?
- LA DOLCE VITA
- THE BUZZ ON BOUTIQUE HOTELS
- SHARE YOUR TRAVELS

FEATURE TRAVEL LINKS

- BROWSE ALL ARTICLES
- CARP TRAVEL
- TRAVEL DISCOUNTS
- CAR RENTAL DISCOUNTS
- TRAVEL CLASSIFIEDS
- VACATION RENTALS

The hobby vacation

Article By: Jennifer Gruden

Indulge your passion for a particular handicraft, take master-level classes and meet others with the same obsession.

When Lisa Edwards, 58, of Toronto started quilting, she expected that she would enjoy the creative and tactile aspects of crafting. What she didn't expect was to find herself loading up the car two years ago for a 12 hour drive south to stay at a B&B and quilt intensively for 5 days.

Or that her husband John would choose to join her – spending his days in the luxurious contemplation of his "endless stack of magazines I haven't read" and walking their 4 year old Golden Retriever through the streets of a sleepy Pennsylvania town. Although the couple originally thought they would have the evenings to explore together, Lisa remembers that she spent her time working ahead for the next class. "Once I got into my project I was determined to finish. John said one night that he felt he was getting a huge break but that I was working harder than he'd seen me work in years."

Welcome to the

Flexible Schedules
Free Seasons Pass
Live the Lifestyle

The hobby vacation combines learning and travel — you get to hone an existing skill or pick up an entirely new one, and do it as part of a holiday. Here again, there are numerous packagers and aggregators who can make it easy to search for the right program — Google returns over one million results.

Sign-up for our newsletters.

HOME PAGE

HEALTH

MONEY

TRAVEL

TODAY'S FEATURE ARTICLES

- LIVE LIKE A KING
- TOP DESTINATIONS FOR WOMEN
- SUN, SEA AND - SURGERY?
- LA DOLCE VITA
- THE BUZZ ON BOUTIQUE HOTELS
- SHARE YOUR TRAVELS

FEATURE TRAVEL LINKS

- BROWSE ALL ARTICLES
- CARP TRAVEL
- TRAVEL DISCOUNTS
- CAR RENTAL DISCOUNTS
- TRAVEL CLASSIFIEDS
- VACATION RENTALS

The ultimate un-cruise

Article By: Cynthia Ross Cravit

Now here's an offbeat cruising option: taking your vacation aboard a working cargo ship.

Just as some cruise lines are offering over-the-top onboard experiences such as water parks, luxury spas, and celebrity chefs, other sorts of cruises are attracting travellers with less flashy ambitions. Far less flashy.

A new off-the-beaten-trail trend to emerge among travellers looking for something different? Un-tourists booking un-cruises – on freighter ships.

While the thought of vacationing alongside shipping containers might not be everyone's idea of a holiday, freighter-enthusiasts are happy to recite the benefits.

Solitude, relaxation, no dress-codes at dinner and costs generally half to a third less than conventional cruises just to name a few. Freighter fares typically range from about $90-$130 (USD) per person per day, inclusive of all meals onboard. Freighter cruises can last from 10 days to 120 days to go around the world.

"We like saying it's like staying

This one looks strange, doesn't it? Taking a cruise on a cargo ship. But it fits the BoomerAging mold — it's offbeat, a little against-the-grain, and is definitely a new kind of experience. Google returned almost 2,000 results — orders of magnitude less than medical tourism, of course, but in my view still a pretty high number for something so new and unusual. It speaks to how quickly the packagers can get at it once they get an inkling of an interesting new niche.

Sign-up for our newsletters.

HOME PAGE

HEALTH

MONEY

TRAVEL

TODAY'S FEATURE ARTICLES

- LIVE LIKE A KING
- TOP DESTINATIONS FOR WOMEN
- SUN, SEA AND - SURGERY?
- LA DOLCE VITA
- THE BUZZ ON BOUTIQUE HOTELS
- SHARE YOUR TRAVELS

FEATURE TRAVEL LINKS

- BROWSE ALL ARTICLES
- CARP TRAVEL
- TRAVEL DISCOUNTS
- CAR RENTAL DISCOUNTS
- TRAVEL CLASSIFIEDS
- VACATION RENTALS

Travel that feeds the soul

Article By: Bonnie Baker Cowan

Becoming a global volunteer allows you to travel the world, contribute skills to help people at risk and connect to another culture.

When Bud Philbrook and Michele Gran were married in 1979, they had chosen a Caribbean cruise as their honeymoon. But during the planning stages, evening newscasts spotlighting the tragic exodus of Cambodians from their terrorized homeland made the couple rethink the frivolity of their honeymoon plans.

They decided then they wanted a more meaningful vacation.

"We spent five days indulging Bud's childhood dream of visiting Orlando theme parks and five days in an impoverished Guatemalan village," says Michele. This blending of fantasy and reality led the couple to a life change that today is exemplified in Global Volunteers, a non-governmental organization (NGO) that supports 20 countries year-round on six continents through volunteer teams, direct project funding and child sponsorship.

Since its inception in 1984, Global Volunteers has sent more than 20,000 volunteers to more than 100

"Voluntourism" is another hot trend, playing into the Boomer desire for new experiences and, at the same time, a dose of altruism and spiritual growth. A host of packagers now exist to help you find exactly the right venue.

These are just four examples of what's going on out there.

There are more extreme examples, too — skydiving, backpacking, scuba diving, safaris, extreme hiking, are all growing categories. Medical tourism has major offshoots in ashram retreats, meditation and detoxification holidays. Long-stay vacations — three months or more — are also a fast-growing category.

For the Boomers, the *experience* is everything. For the travel industry, this produces a *permanent* need to create, package and promote an ever-widening range of those experiences. The image of a bus-load of docile "seniors," obediently wobbling into a museum, listening to a few words from their guide, and then climbing back on to the bus, is fast being obliterated by the go-anywhere, do-anything mindset that drives BoomerAging.

Housing

As far as Boomers are concerned, they are *never* going into a nursing home. In fact, the antipathy toward nursing homes — and all the associated images of helplessness, loss of dignity and possibly even abuse — extends to those much older than Boomers. According to "Aging in Place," a study commissioned by Clarity and the EAR Foundation, released in October 2007, "Senior citizens fear moving into a nursing home and losing their independence more than death." 82% of Boomers feared their parents would be mistreated in a nursing home; 89% worried their parents would feel depressed.

And their parents' views, as tracked in the study, supported those worries. Asked to state their greatest fear, 26% of seniors cited loss of independence; 13% specifically cited having to move out of their house and into a nursing home. By contrast, only 3% said "death" was their greatest fear.

And if that's what the Boomers are worried about, vis-à-vis their parents, all the more so are they determined not to let it happen to themselves.

That's why "aging in place" or "independent living" is becoming such a hot topic: Boomers want it, their parents want it, and it certainly suits government policy makers terrified at the prospect of having nursing homes and hospitals overrun by a coming tidal wave of old people.

The trouble is, the very nature of "the home" has to change in order to make all this possible. Without renovation — and new technology — the traditional home in which most Boomers live is not always a suitable environment for aging. It gets harder to climb those stairs, reach under those kitchen counters, avoid slipping and falling. By your 40s — certainly by your 50s — there can be issues of mobility, safety and comfort.

Fortunately — and not surprisingly, given the size of the market — industry is responding with a host of new products and services, all designed to make it easier and safer to stay in one's home for longer. Boomers are only just beginning to become aware of these products, and to spend money on them; the long-term trend is irresistible, and it should benefit, among others, home improvement specialty retailers like The Home Depot, Lowe's and others.

At the simple end of the scale, we have an upgrading of basic elements: those ugly metal safety bars that are bolted into showers and baths, like an afterthought (which is exactly what they were, up until now), have been replaced by sleek new designs that build the safety features in and make a seamless "fashion statement." No more retro-fitting of utilitarian aids that shout, "Look what I had to do — I'm getting old." Now these features are designed in, right from the start.

Moen Products, a leading manufacturer of faucets, sinks and kitchen and bathroom accessories, conducted consumer research on the subject. "These bath safety products traditionally have had an institutional look and feel, and were sold primarily through pharmacies or medical equipment dealers," Moen said in a 2005 press release on the project. Moen "set out to shift that paradigm, learning directly from consumers what they need, want or just plain like in bath assistive devices — and to make it easier to find and purchase them." Moen and Creative Specialties International (CSI), its bath accessories division, conducted in-depth interviews in the home, probing participants' physical needs, but also their lifestyles. They found a lot of enthusiasm for the idea of combining safety and style. Now they promote the products that way. The products are presented as a "collection," and the word "designer" is frequently used.

From the bathroom to the entire house, the idea is emerging that new approaches to design will be necessary — and that a substantial market will pay for them. One interesting idea is the Universal Design movement (sometimes called Flex Design), which seeks to make barrier-free homes a new paradigm. The idea is that the home should have the safety/comfort features that will be required for aging designed into place right from the beginning, so that the home can flexibly respond — with minimum additional cost — to the evolving physical needs of the owners. Universal design features include

- At least one entrance that does not require stairs
- Wide interior doors and hallways (minimum 36 inches)
- Lever handles, instead of twisting knobs, for opening doors
- Light switches with flat panels instead of small toggle switches
- Brighter lighting
- Ramp access

- Non-slip flooring
- Low-maintenance exterior and interior finishes
- Low-maintenance landscape

The National Association of Home Builders in the USA has developed a program to certify builders in these designs and techniques (Certified Aging in Place Specialist). In Canada, there's a Universal Design Institute associated with the University of Manitoba. The UK's Design Council promotes many of the same ideas under the banner of "inclusive design."

Coming next: a host of high-tech features to make the home even more comfortable and convenient. A good description of the "home of the future" is found in "Eternal Youths," a report on Boomers published in 2004 in the UK, by Demos Research:

> The idea of the purpose-built, technologically-advanced SMART-HOME has excited academics and futuroloists for some years, and is a good example of an assistive technology which might be ideally suited to the material and aesthetic needs of Baby Boomers. In the average prototypical SMARTHOME, for example, small motors and sensors are fitted to moveable objects around the house and are operated by a single infrared controller. Doors, windows and curtains can be automatically opened to varying degrees; sinks and cupboards, mounted on lifting mechanisms, can be raised to optimally accessible heights; baths and sinks can be filled to particular levels at specific temperatures; lights can be turned on and off from a distance.
>
> In the SMARTHOME, sophisticated technology can take the hard work out of household maintenance. Take the Robomower, an automatic lawnmower that cuts grass, mulches it up into powder and leaves the remains on the lawn as a natural fertiliser. Or the Electromelt system, a network of heating cables, which melts snow and ice on driveways.

Or why not a robot to do it all for you? This recent article on our website generated thousands of clicks immediately:

The robot will see you now

Article By: Cynthia Ross Cravit

It sounds like the stuff of science fiction – but could we become as dependent on robots as on our personal computers?

Robots are already a part of society, particularly in manufacturing, industry and the military. But what about robots as teachers, housekeepers, caregivers and even surgeons?

In all of these cases it's already starting to happen. A super-advanced droid named Tiro, for example, recently assisted a human instructor with an English class at Euon Primary School in South Korea. Aside from a few glitches (Tiro fell silent for a few moments after the computer she was connected to had problems), the experiment gave a glimpse of what a futuristic classroom could look like in this high-wired country.

Korean researchers say networked robots such as Tiro could be used to facilitate a child's education by, among other things, relaying messages to parents, teaching languages – and when the kids become bored, even sing and dance for them. Outside the home, a robot could be used to guide customers at post offices or

50Plus.com

Sign-up for our newsletters.

HOME PAGE

HEALTH

MONEY

TRAVEL

LIFESTYLE

TODAY'S FEATURE ARTICLES

- A FACELIFT IN THE FRIDGE?
- PILATES, PLEASE
- NOVEMBER GARDENING TIPS
- LEGENDS AND FRIENDS
- ADD ROMANCE TO YOUR HOME
- COOKING FOR YOUR PET

FEATURE LIFESTYLE LINKS

- BROWSE ALL ARTICLES
- FAMILY CIRCLE
- NEWSLETTER
- GARDENING
- MEALS MADE EASY
- RECIPES
- ARTHUR BLACK

Honda's ASIMO robot, referred to in the article, is already being touted as having the potential to provide caregiving services.

The entire house itself may become a "living" part of the action, rather than a passive — albeit much more benign — environment. Intel is researching "the digital home," in which a network of electronic devices deliver health and wellness services. Some of the details were discussed in a paper by Eric Dishman, Intel's General Manager of Health Research and Innovation, at a 2006 conference I attended, sponsored by AARP:

> Intel has made a substantial investment in R&D to advance the concept of the digital home, in which computers and consumer electronic (CE) devices throughout the home are linked together in a wireless network. Once the digital home infrastructure is in place, any computer or CE device could also be used to deliver health and wellness applications. Older adults will be able to access these applications through whatever interfaces are most familiar to them, from phones to PCs to televisions; they will not have to learn new technology. The goal is to have a variety of interfaces distributed throughout the home, within easy reach of the person needing assistance.

An additional feature of the digital home will be the ability to conduct constant diagnosis and leverage the feedback into proactive assistance. This will not only help the resident, but distant caregivers (i.e., Boomers worrying about their parents).

> A variety of technologies in the digital home will enable older adults to age in place, improving the quality of their lives and reducing health care costs by deferring expensive institutional care. Existing telemedicine technologies can access data from the digital home network, enabling virtual exams in the home. Proactive computing technologies under research at Intel and elsewhere will reduce costs further by enabling the aging to be proactive about caring for themselves. A network of sensors throughout the digital home will track and monitor health status and activities of older adults, providing input for proactive applications that will offer a variety of assistance, from reminders to take medications to help in completing cooking tasks and accessing social support. Seniors will access the network using a variety of familiar

interfaces, such as telephones and televisions; they will not need to learn new technology to receive assistance. Such proactive systems will also enable adult children to assess the health and well-being of their aging parents remotely through private, secure Internet connections and will provide on-site caregivers with the social support they need to avoid burnout — a common problem among caregivers of older adults.

Since many of these exciting developments are some time into the future, it's fair to ask if Boomers are already spending big on home improvement. The answer is a very strong "Yes!"

· According to a 2005 report from Harvard's Joint Center for Housing Studies, Boomers continue to dominate "every aspect of the US housing market, from rentals to starter homes to tradeup homes and remodeling." Even as the Boomers get older and become "Empty Nesters," notes the report, "the Baby Boomers do not appear to be in a rush to downsize their homes or stop making extensive home improvements. Indeed, six in ten Baby Boomers completed a home improvement project in 2002–2003, raising their total inflation-adjusted spending from $17 billion in 1995 to $72 billion. Even today, three decades after first appearing on the housing scene, Baby Boomers still account for more than half of all remodeling expenditures and more than 60% of all spending on room additions."

· According to Abbey Bank's *Lifestyle Report*, in 2007 British Boomers spent 10 times as much per week on home improvement as the 65+ generation, and more than any other age group.

· In Canada, Boomers spend more on home renovation than any other age group, in every category of spending. For example, Boomers account for nearly 40% of the market for projects that cost more than $20,000.

As industry rushes to produce more safety and convenience products, and new technologies come on stream, these trends will only strengthen. The Boomers are already fighting to keep their parents out of institutions for as long as possible, and when it comes to themselves, they're even more determined to "age in place."

Technology

Many of the products and services that Boomers are purchasing, and will purchase, involve the latest in technology. As we saw in our analysis of "oldness," aging has traditionally been characterized by an *under*utilization of technology. The image of an "old-timer" who is befuddled by a "new-fangled" gadget is a comedy staple.

But the Boomers, remember, were the yuppies of the 1970s — not only tech-savvy, but tech-driven: they *had* to have the newest toys, whatever those toys were. And there is no sign of this changing now.

The TVLand network, which specifically targets Boomers, recently completed a research study on the topic. Appropriately titled *The Joy of Tech*, the study focused on media techologies, but I believe the results are valid across the widest possible range of products and services.

The study reports, "Boomers have the numbers, financial means and desire to create their 'digital nest' — a place where new media technology is employed to create both a personal escape and as well as an entertainment hub for family and friends." The study confirmed the clear difference between Boomers and previous generations: "Unlike older generations, Boomers feel that they are youthful enough to fully embrace and be comfortable with technology, but not too young to take for granted the positive changes technology has brought to the world, as younger 'tech native' generations do."

"It's clear that Boomers love technology," said TVLand president Larry W. Jones, commenting on the study. "We know that 65% of Boomers have tried a new technology in the last three years. *The Joy of Tech* study shows us that Boomers are flocking to these new devices to give them control over and enhance their quality of life. This is the generation that made status symbols out of cars and they are doing the same thing with new media products using high-tech home theater systems and other tech products to define who they are."

Not surprisingly, the study found that most Boomers aren't bothered by the high costs that can sometimes attach — at least initially — to new technologies. To the contrary, they are prepared to spend more than younger generations — and they have the money to do so. HDTV, TIVO and DVR, VOD, online TV . . . Boomers are heavy consumers of new media technologies.

What's important about all of these trends is that they speak to the *attitudes* that characterize BoomerAging — in direct contrast with "oldness." You may find the table below to be a little ruthless; I submit that it's completely accurate.

The Old Old	The New Old
"I'm running out of gas" I don't have the energy to keep track of all these new things. It isn't expected of me; everybody understands I'm a senior citizen on a fixed income.	**"I've still got it"** I always controlled the market, and have the energy, the interest and the clout. (And I've always been measured by how much stuff I had — you think I'm going to retreat *now*?)
"This is all new to me" All these new trends, these new products, I can't keep track of it all. It's a whole different world out there; I feel like a stranger to most of it.	**"This is me"** I've always been the leader — the first to pursue what's new, what's hot, what's interesting. Being engaged is literally who I am.
"I don't have enough time" It might be nice for me to be able to make sense out of all this — but let's face it, I'm not going to be around for that much longer.	**"I have plenty of time"** I'm going to live to 100 — maybe longer! I have plenty of time to learn, shop, buy and use all of the exciting new stuff.
"This isn't going to help me" Maybe if I were 20 years younger . . .	**"I want *everything* that will make my life better"** I want everything that will *keep* me young, and help me enjoy who I really am.
"And besides . . . who can afford it?"	**"If I can't pay cash, I can always use plastic"**

Looking ahead to future generations — does anyone seriously believe that the children and the grandchildren of the Boomers (and generations beyond them) will revert to column one?

Ever again?

The most dramatic contrast between "oldness" and BoomerAging is on the topic of . . . surprise, surprise . . . sex.

Not that sex and "oldness" were ever completely disconnected. But in the "oldness" construct, sex was reserved for men, and it was associated with something not quite right — sometimes portrayed as humorous, sometimes as distasteful. The image of the "dirty old man" was a cliché of both drama and comedy.

In the movie *Grumpy Old Men*, Jack Lemmon's character, a 60-something widower, boasts about how much "pipe" he has "laid," but is all fumbles with the still-lovely Ann-Margret. Meanwhile, Lemmon's 94-year-old father, played by Burgess Meredith, talks incessantly about sex and ridicules his son's lack of progress. All this is right on target as a representation of the traditional view of "oldness."

But it's absolutely *not* how the Boomers are experiencing things.

Let's make the easy point first. Boomer men are certainly as interested in sex as Jack Lemmon's "grumpy old man" character, but they definitely don't see themselves as old or uncertain — they wouldn't assume, as Lemmon's character did, that the Ann-Margret character was out of their reach. That said, even in the "oldness" scheme of things, men were assumed to be always thinking about sex. So while "dirty old man" might evolve into "sexy" player, the underlying fundamentals aren't all that different.

The more interesting point is what's happened to the *female* side of the relationship.

In the world of "oldness," women were supposed to be finished as sexual "players" by their 50s — certainly by their 60s. The operating cliché was that of the 50ish or 60ish husband landing his roving eye on the hot young secretary and leaving his dutiful Pleasantville wife, who had no choice but to suck it up. There was no way she could compete with a sweet young thing, and if Hubby let his hormones wreck their 25-year marriage, she was just out of luck.

Those days are gone forever.

We get a good clue, interestingly, from the same movie that portrayed the "grumpy old" Jack Lemmon. For all his bragging, he never gets up the nerve to make a serious move on the Ann-Margret character, a 50-ish widow. No, it's *she* who makes the move on *him* — much to his astonishment. There's this almost glazed smile on his face, this stunned look of "I can't believe this is happening to me" as she smoothly, and without any fuss or embarrassment, gets him into bed.

Best-selling author Gail Sheehy began tracking women through their life stages in her groundbreaking book, *Passages*, published in 1976. Thirty years and several books later, she published *Sex and the Seasoned Woman*, in which hundreds of Baby Boomer — and older — women spoke to her with astonishing candor about their sex lives.

> *Sex and the Seasoned Woman* is a book about a new universe of lusty, liberated women, some married and some not, who are unwilling to settle for the stereotypical roles of middle age . . .
>
> A seasoned woman is spicy. She has been marinated in life experience. Like a complex wine, she can be alternately sweet, tart, sparkling, mellow. She is both maternal and playful. Assured, alluring, and resourceful. She is less likely to have an agenda than a young woman — no biological clock tick-tocking beside her lover's bed, no campaign to lead him to the altar, no rescue fantasies. The seasoned woman knows who she is. She could be any one of us, as long as she is committed to living fully and passionately in the second half of her life, despite failures and false starts.
>
> Margaret, an old friend and former radical who was still married to her only husband and living in rural New Hampshire, confided to me how shocked she was to hear stories from her contemporary female friends who are divorced or widowed in their sixties or seventies. "They're having romantic escapades with young guys, they talk about erotic discoveries, a couple of them have fallen in love again, but they

want relationships beyond conventional marriage." Margaret still thought of herself as the free spirit who had walked the wild side in the 1960s. "I was the rebel, and they were the stick-in-the-muds. Now I'm the old married fuddyduddy."

But you do not have to break up your marriage to change your life. Long-married women are also waking up to the possibilities of postmenopausal sensuality and proposing new contracts to shake the staleness out of their relationships and release their deferred creative energies.

Just how old is a seasoned woman? I define it very much the way Auntie Mame's friend Vera did when asked, "How old are you, anyway?"

"Somewhere between forty and death."

It's not over at 45 or 50, "it" being sex, intimacy, discovery of a new identity and a new passion in life. On the contrary, it begins all over again.

To measure the extent of the trend, the *New England Journal of Medicine* conducted 3,005 two-hour interviews with men and women aged 57 to 85. The results were summarized in an article on our website, "Those sexy seniors."

The survey found that a significant number of both men and women reported being sexually active well into their 70s and 80s.

According to the survey, the barriers to sex, if any, had more to do with health problems or lack of a partner, rather than age. Sex with a partner in the previous year was reported by

- 73% of those aged 57 to 64
- 53% of those aged 64 to 75
- 26% of those aged 75 to 85

The article generated a huge number of clicks and many interesting comments in the reader response box that we put under all our articles. Here are just a few . . .

Great! Let's keep doing it!! From still doing it age 63!! — Valerie

Whew! Do I ever consider myself lucky. I am in a monogamous relationship with my partner of four years! We met on the internet and although he is married (his wife languishes in a nursing home and has done for over ten years) we are very much in love. We have regular sex more than once a week and it is the best sex I have ever had! I think the fact that we are totally commited to one another makes it so good. Love WITH sex is wonderful. I thank God for him every day. He's faithful, loving, kind and considerate and when the right time comes, we will be married. I just had to share this with your readers. Do not give up the hope of finding a loving partner, no matter your age. — Gracie

"Let's keep doing it," advises 63-year-old Valerie. And that was certainly the strategy of Jane Juska. A retired English teacher in California, single parent, divorced for 30 years, in the fall of 1999 she placed this ad in the *New York Times Review of Books:*

Before I turn 67 — next March — I would like to have a lot of sex with a man I like. If you want to talk first, Trollope works for me.

Inundated with responses, she carefully chose a few men, flew to New York, and proceeded to have enough romantic adventures to fill two books: *A Round-Heeled Woman: My Late-Life Adventures in Sex and Romance*, followed by *Unaccompanied Women: Late-Life Adventures in Love, Sex and Real Estate*. The books became best-sellers, and Juska found herself jetting all over North America and Europe for book signings and interviews.

In 2007, Juska gave an exclusive interview to my wife, Cynthia, who is (a) a Baby Boomer, (b) exceptionally beautiful and sexy and (c) the Editorial Director of our company's flagship website, www.5oplus.com.

"When I placed the ad," Juska told Cynthia, "I meant what it said: I wanted to have a lot of sex with a man I liked. I did not think that good sex need be accompanied by love; affection and friendship can do as well, perhaps even better. I do not think sex can be casual; it is an act with profound consequences. When people claim to have casual sex, they are saying they are having not particularly good sex or even bad sex and they don't want to think about it. I fell in love almost immediately with a man who didn't love me back; the sex was awful. The best sex I had was with a man I was not in love with but whom I liked enormously; and with a man I adored but who was 32 so love was out of the question, or so I thought."

It's worth noting that Juska was 74 when this interview took place — older than the oldest Baby Boomer, of course, but definitely displaying the mindset of Boomers: a frankness about what she wants; a determination to pursue those wants, regardless of previously accepted norms or taboos; a willingness to talk about the experience without any embarrassment.

"I was as self-conscious as anyone about my body," she told Cynthia, "especially with the man who was 32. But he was persistent, gently so, and I didn't want to get to be 90 and kick myself for having turned him down. So I hid under a lot of covers. He didn't, though."

Even though she's a decade or so older than the oldest Boomer, Juska's explanation of what motivated her is classic Boomer thinking: "I was willing to risk everything in my search for living fully."

This article produced — and continues to produce — a huge number of clicks, and readers' comments were largely very supportive. Most of the comments came from women, and you get the sense that they were excited to have the opportunity to declare their own sexuality.

Sign-up for our newsletters.

HOME PAGE

HEALTH

MONEY

TRAVEL

LIFESTYLE

TODAY'S FEATURE ARTICLES

- ◆ UNIQUE GIFT IDEAS
- ◆ DECK THE HALLS
- ◆ SEEKING THE SANDMAN
- ◆ HIP AT 100
- ◆ MIX UP THE HOLIDAYS
- ◆ ONLINE SHOPPING

FEATURE LIFESTYLE LINKS

- ◆ BROWSE ALL ARTICLES
- ◆ FAMILY CIRCLE
- ◆ NEWSLETTER
- ◆ GARDENING
- ◆ MEALS MADE EASY
- ◆ RECIPES
- ◆ ARTHUR BLACK

A round-heeled woman

Article By: Cynthia Ross Cravit

Sexy at 70: who says you have to be young to have a fulfilling sex life?

Before I turn 67 - next March - I would like to have a lot of sex with a man I like. If you want to talk first, Trollope works for me.

This is the personal ad that former English teacher Jane Juska placed in the *New York Times Book Review* back in fall of 1999. And now, at 74, she's had enough romantic adventures to fill two books: *A Round-Heeled Woman: My Late-Life Adventures in Sex and Romance* and more recently, *Unaccompanied Women: Late-Life Adventures in Love, Sex and Real Estate*. (For those not in the know, a 'round-heeled woman' is an old-time slang expression for a woman who is promiscuous.)

Judging by the popularity of her books, Juska – who has been divorced for over 30 years and is a single parent – has apparently struck a resonant chord among women and men seeking romantic and sexual

fulfillment into their 60s and beyond. A blossoming literary career has her jetting all

Have read both books — excellent!

Good on ya, Jane!! I thought I was brave to come to China to teach English at 58, but that's nothing compared to your adventures! I'll look for your books when I'm back home; sounds like an interesting read! — Jilly

I haven't read these books yet but am on my way out the door to buy both if I can get them. Good for you. I don't know if I would have the courage to do what you did but I admire your "go for it" attitude. — Sue

Hi . . . I'm sending this e-mail to my sister, she told me I was crazy to get married at 60, the reason was that people did not have sex at my age. She also told me that I should see a doctor, that I must be sick because I told her I wanted to have a sex life. Guess I have a lot of company because I'm not alone. Right. P.S. I married a man 10 years younger than myself. — Hot Cookie

Considering the minor pleasure of some sex and the major health and safety risks there are to be taken, I consider the venture to be pretty much stupid. — Voltar

Enjoy Jane! Most women are not interested after 60 years old or not interested in new lovers. I am 76 & still love it. — dingaling

The Boomer attitude toward sexuality isn't just a North American thing — it's also in abundant evidence in the UK. A 2007 survey conducted for wanobe.com, a UK lifestyle site for 50-plus Boomers, revealed that sex on a first date is twice as likely for singles over 50 than for their under-40 counterparts.

The poll, of more than 1,000 men and women between the ages of 50 and 65, was conducted by Wanobe in partnership with Europe's largest online dating service, PARSHIP. It found that 37% of singles over 60 would have sex on a first date — compared to just 18% of under-40s.

Other interesting highlights:

- 53% of the over-50 singles said lust and passion were more important than marriage. In fact, only 7% were hoping that their next relationship would result in marriage — compared to 32% of singles in their 30s.
- 73% of over-50 singles were hoping for a fulfilling sexual relationship in the coming 12 months; 84% were hoping for a fulfilling sexual relationship with the *next person they met!*
- 60% said they didn't care what their children thought of their dates.

"The idea that this age group is no longer interested in a sexual relationship is simply a misconception," said Dr. Victoria Lukats, a psychiatrist and relationship expert for PARSHIP, in a press release on the study.

I'm sure it hasn't escaped your notice that it was an online dating service that co-sponsored the research. Internet dating perfectly demonstrates the impact of BoomerAging: the combination of lust, convenience, control and technology. The Internet makes it fast, easy, safe, anonymous (until you're ready) and very convenient (a huge selection, and the opportunity to be very specific right off the bat). Not surprisingly, the 50-plus age group is now the hottest growth segment of the online dating market.

My company's flagship site, www.50plus.com, has a thriving dating section in partnership with industry leader Lavalife:

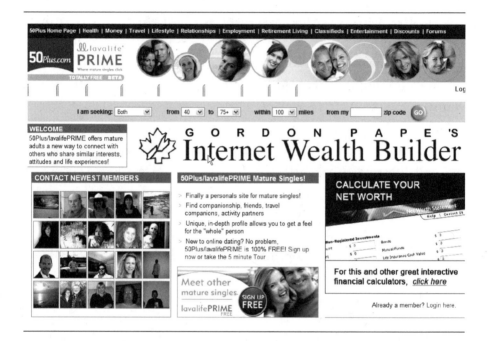

Just for fun, on March 22, 2008, I conducted a search, looking for women aged 60 to 75, within 100 miles of my postal code:

The search returned over 21 pages of results.

Our partner Lavalife is one of the biggest dating sites, but the landscape is certainly crowded . . . as Google shows.

Google   Web   Images   Groups   News   Maps   Scholar   more »
boomers online dating   [Search]   Advanced Search / Preferences
Search: ⊙ the web ○ pages from Canada

Web   Results 1 - 10 of about 1,270,000 for boomers online dating. (0.15 s

eHarmony® **Online Dating**   Sponsored Link
www.eHarmony.ca   Looking for a Serious Relationship? Let eHarmony Help. Free Profile!

Baby **Boomer Dating** Site Providing Senior **Online Dating** Sites Where ...
Baby Boomer Dating Site Your Center For Baby Boomer Online Dating Where Boomers
and Seniors Find Love and Romance.
www.babyboomerdatingsite.com/ - 13k - Cached - Similar pages - Note this

> Baby **Boomer Dating** Blog: Baby **Boomer Online Dating** Site
> As I said in my last post, I agree with some of the new online dating membership sites that
> refer to Boomers as "seniors", but I still think there should be ...
> www.babyboomerdatingsite.com/blog/2006/09/baby-boomer-online-dating-site.html - 15k -
> Cached - Similar pages - Note this
> [More results from www.babyboomerdatingsite.com]

5 Rules for **Online Dating** Over 50 - MSN Lifestyle: **Boomers**
Online dating may seem like an obvious route for younger generations, but a single guy
friend of mine who's in his fifties recently voiced his objection to ...
boomers.msn.com/articleOP.aspx?cp-documentid=376647 - 23k -
Cached - Similar pages - Note this

Amazon.ca: **Boomer's** Guide to **Online Dating**: Books: Judsen Culbreth
Amazon.ca: Boomer's Guide to Online Dating: Books: Judsen Culbreth by Judsen Culbreth.
www.amazon.ca/Boomers-Online-Dating-Judsen-Culbreth/dp/1594862257 - 70k -
Cached - Similar pages - Note this

blognation Canada » Blog Archive » LavalifePRIME Brings **Online** ...
Source: lavalifePRIME BLENDS SOCIAL NETWORKING and ONLINE DATING. It seems to
be a fact of the baby boomer generation that divorce and social monogamy

Sponsored Links

Lavalife: Sex in the City
Where Singles Click.
Lavalife Official Site. Join Free.
Lavalife.com

Dating
More than 4 million members.
Get a Free Matchmaking Profile!
www.be2.ca
Ontario

On Line Dating
Find Your Perfect Match At The One
& Only Perfectmatch.com. Start Now!
www.Perfectmatch.com

100% Free Dating
No Credit Card Required.
Email Local Singles Free.
SinglesNet.com

Elite Millionaire **Dating**
Seen on DR PHIL! Join to find
Wealthy Men & Gorgeous Women.
www.SugarDaddie.com

100% Free Dating

Google   Web   Images   Groups   News   Maps   Scholar   more »
seniors online dating   [Search]   Advanced Search / Preferences
Search: ⊙ the web ○ pages from Canada

Web   Results 1 - 10 of about 4,050,000 for seniors online dating. (0.13

50+ Digital Marketing   Sponsored Links
www.immersionactive.com   Specialized in boomers and seniors. Download our latest whitepaper.

Lavalife: **Online Dating**
Lavalife.com   Chat With Like-Minded People. Join Free: Where Singles Click.

Senior Dating in Canada
www.Date.ca   Meet interesting singles at the top senior social network in Canada

Senior FriendFinder - **Online** Personals and **Senior Dating** for ...
482 Members Online!*. 451532 Total Members!*. Search for Singles! I am a: Man, Woman,
Couple, Group. seeking a: Man, Woman, Couple (man and woman) ...
seniorfriendfinder.com/ - 29k - Cached - Similar pages - Note this

Senior Mates: senior dating, senior online dating, senior dating ...
Login to the world of Senior Mates.Here at seniormates.com you will encounter people who
are sincerely looking to meet other senior persons.
www.seniormates.com/ - 22k - Cached - Similar pages - Note this

Site is down for maintenance
Site is down for maintenance.
www.thedatingsenior.com/ - 1k - Cached - Similar pages - Note this

Senior Dating, **Senior Sex**, and **Senior** Romance
Whether you're in a relationship or wish you were, here are some resources to keep you
informed on the issues of senior dating, senior sex, and romance ...
seniorliving.about.com/od/sexromance/For_Seniors_Dating_Sex_Romance.htm - 17k -
Cached - Similar pages - Note this

Sponsored Links

100% Free Dating
Adults Looking for Flirt
Join Now & Meet Someone Today!
www.Dating-FlirtGame.com

Free **Dating**
No Credit Card Required.
Email Local Singles Free.
www.SinglesNet.com

Free **Senior Dating**
Meet Single Seniors Seeking Love.
View Profiles 100% Free. Join Now!
www.DatingForSeniors.com

Free **Dating** - Fitness
View Photo Profiles. Local Singles
into Fitness. Join Now for Free.
www.Fitness-Singles.com

The Allied Network
Visit our Website for a Free Date.
The Right Person Is Waiting For You
www.thealliednetwork.com
Ontario

100% Free Dating

Google   Web   Images   Groups   News   Maps   Scholar   more »
seniors sex   [Search]   Advanced Search / Preferences
Search: ⊙ the web ○ pages from Canada

Web   Results 1 - 10 of about 1,940,000 for seniors sex. (0.1

Senior Dating in Canada   Sponsored Links
www.Date.ca   Meet interesting singles at the top senior social network in Canada

Lavalife: Online Dating
Lavalife.com   Chat With Like-Minded People. Join Free: Where Singles Click.

Senior Sex - 6 Steps to Better **Senior Sex**
With creativity and communication, you can continue to improve your sex life as you age.
Here are 6 steps to help make senior sex better.
seniorliving.about.com/od/sexromance/ss/6step_seniorsex.htm - 21k -
Cached - Similar pages - Note this

> **Senior** Dating, **Senior Sex**, and **Senior** Romance
> Whether you're in a relationship or wish you were, information for seniors on senior dating,
> senior sex and senior romance.
> seniorliving.about.com/od/sexromance/For_Seniors_Dating_Sex_Romance.htm - 17k -
> Cached - Similar pages - Note this
> [More results from seniorliving.about.com]

Sex for **Senior** Citizens - SeniorJournal.com
5. 2007 - Health and lifestyle matter when it comes to a health sex life, particularly for senior
citizens, too often plagued by various health issues. ...
seniorjournal.com/Sex.htm - 112k - Cached - Similar pages - Note this

Sex and **Senior** Citizens
sex and senior citizens. ... Bulletins -- news and bulletins on sex for and by seniors. ... Web
Resources -- on sex after 50. Products --for seniors ...
seniors-site.com/sex/ - 13k - Cached - Similar pages - Note this

Sponsored Links

Over 50 Active Dating
View Photo Profiles. Meet Local
Active Singles. Join Now for Free.
www.Fitness-Singles.com

Date Single **Senior** Women
Meet Sexy Single Seniors
1000s of Local Profiles. Join Now!
www.SeniorDateLink.com

Online Dating for Free
Meet Canadian Singles Now!
Search Photos and Profiles
www.Ca-Singles.com

Free **Senior** Dating
Meet local senior singles free.
Limited time offer. Join today!
100percentfreedating.com/senior.htm

Meet & Date Singles
Looking for singles in your area?
Browse profiles, chat & more.
www.metrodate.ca

100% Free Dating
Email Local Singles For Free

Millions of references, pointing to thousands of websites, aggregators of websites, sellers of products and services, all catering to a huge army of Boomers and seniors, all of them on the prowl, looking for love in all the right, wrong or digital places.

A 2006 article in *Newsweek* reported on the importance of this market segment to the online dating industry: "Early on, dating sites were for the young and reckless — who *knew* what kind of creeps were out there? — but now, as Internet dating has become more established and the number of people joining sites has leveled off, single boomers are a hot commodity. The number of boomers visiting Lavalife.com, a site known for its young and urban clientele, has grown 39% over the last three years,

Along with dating connections, there's a hunger for information. The majority of these folks, after all, have been out of the dating scene for decades. At www.50plus.com, we have an entire section devoted to relationships. Here are some of the articles we featured on just one day (March 22, 2008):

- BEHAVIOURS
- BOUNDRIES
- CARDS
- CASINO
- CLUBS
- COLD SHOULDER
- COMING OUT
- CUPIDS KEYBOARD
- VIEW ALL TOPICS

EMPLOYMENT

RETIREMENT LIVING

CLASSIFIEDS

ENTERTAINMENT

DISCOUNTS

FORUMS

BLOGS

CONTESTS

SIGN-IN

SEARCH
RELATIONSHIPS

search

Retirement Communities
Information, listings & free advice.

50Plus 50Plus.com
Community Forums
See what thousands of visitors are talking about right now!

Mistaking sex for love
While the act of sex is certainly lovely, it's not necessarily love.
Continue

The male boomer and long-term relationships
Both men and women are short changed when sweeping generalizations are applied to the male psyche. Continue

Affairs online
The Internet makes it easy to connect with other people... sometimes *too* easy. Continue

Untying the knot: where to start

Our site enables readers to comment on the articles, and to dialogue with each other. The discussions are often very vigorous. Here's what the pre-nup article looked like:

50Plus.com

Sign-up for our newsletters.

HOME PAGE

HEALTH

MONEY

TRAVEL

LIFESTYLE

RELATIONSHIPS
TODAY'S FEATURE ARTICLES

- THE DATING GAME
- MISTAKING SEX FOR LOVE
- THE MALE BOOMER
- AN AFFAIR, VIRTUALLY
- UNTYING THE KNOT
FEATURE RELATIONSHIPS LINKS
- SIGN-IN
- BROWSE ALL ARTICLES
- JOIN TODAY
SEARCH RELATIONSHIPS TOPICS

- ATTITUDES
- AWKWARD
- BEHAVIOURS
- BOUNDRIES
- CARDS
- CASINO
- CLUBS
- COLD SHOULDER
- COMING OUT
- CUPIDS KEYBOARD
- VIEW ALL TOPICS

Do you need a pre-nup?

Article By: Jennifer Gruden

Even if you're sure you've finally found the right partner, you should consider how to protect yourself financially.

Second marriages can be very different from first marriages. Couples may feel "older but wiser" and be sure that this time, they've gotten it right – and won't be headed for divorce court. And to some extent, they're right – Canadian statistics suggest when both members of a couple are over 40 and entering a second marriage, they face only half as great a risk of marital dissolution as those who were under 30.

Even so, that rate may be as high as 27 per cent, or one quarter of all second marriages. And since older couples tend to have accumulated more personal assets before they come into a marriage – divorce settlements, home equity, investment savings and earnings, and inheritances, for example – they may have more to loose if the marriage dissolves.

So even if you're sure that you've finally found the right partner, you should consider how best to protect yourself financially. In Canada there is no question that a prenuptial agreement can be one of the best ways to ensure that

Bored of your usual **walk?**

Immunizations for Travel Abroad

Special Education Feature

Diarrhea is the most frequent cause of illness in people who travel to developing countries. Dukoral is an oral vaccine licensed in Canada to help prevent Travellers? Diarrhea.
Read More

Livtopia Opens Latin American Real Estate Marketplace

Advertising Feature

Buying a dream home in Latin America is easier and safer than ever!
Read More

The article generated more than 50 reader comments; here's just a tiny sample:

Certainly do not believe such an exercise to be fearful. Educating oneself should not be fearful. Assets going into any relationship remain the property of the holder. They are only shared if combined and appreciation is shared equally. Inheritances are generally excluded unless shared or combined. For material items it is always good to express in writing your desire to keep this as a family item. Matrimonial homes are shared equally, unless expressed, why not in a prenup. Sunset clause is a great idea. — Felix

Don't forget that cohabitation agreements are just as important for couples who decide to live common law. I live in Manitoba and after the changes to the property laws in June 2004, my partner and I signed a cohabitation agreement to protect our assets accumulated prior to living together. www.gov.mb.ca/justice/family/commonlaw/index.html
—Suitsoff

If you are still living in a country that is in the dark ages and doesn't recognize gay marriage, there will be no problem. The partner would be considered a tenant and he can be booted out by the sheriff. It would be the same as 2 best friends living together and getting in a fight. I am ready for a new partner. — Mike

I have never been married and if I will a pre-nup would be excellent especially if he has more assets than me. That is to be fair to him.
— Ebkin

The article about online affairs was, not surprisingly, more provocative . . .

Sign-up for our newsletters.

HOME PAGE

HEALTH

MONEY

TRAVEL

LIFESTYLE

RELATIONSHIPS

TODAY'S FEATURE ARTICLES

- THE DATING GAME
- DO YOU NEED A PRE-NUP?
- MISTAKING SEX FOR LOVE
- THE MALE BOOMER
- UNTYING THE KNOT

FEATURE RELATIONSHIPS LINKS

- SIGN-IN
- BROWSE ALL ARTICLES
- JOIN TODAY

SEARCH RELATIONSHIPS TOPICS

- ATTITUDES
- AWKWARD
- BEHAVIOURS
- BOUNDRIES
- CARDS
- CASINO
- CLUBS
- COLD SHOULDER
- COMING OUT

Affairs online

Article By: Jennifer Gruden

The Internet makes it easy to connect with other people... sometimes *too* easy.

Looking back, Grace* remembers many cozy evenings at home after her youngest son went to school, she sitting in front of the television knitting and her husband playing games on his computer.

She writes on a divorce support email list: "I never thought much of it. We would talk sometimes with us both in the room. But then I started to notice that he would hide screens when I came by.... Then came the 'classic' signs where he got new clothes and lost some weight and just started acting different.... Still I didn't want to know and besides I told myself he was home with me every night."

The Internet has provided many ways to connect with other people... sometimes too easy of a way. As Grace found out, some 'net relationships can be very intense.

"Then one night he told me that he had met someone that truly understood him and that he was confused and unhappy in our marriage. I don't even know how they met each other.... I told

NEW WAVE MUD BATH?
BOG SNORKELLING?

Yoga for golfers

More golfers are looking to the 5,000-year-old practice of yoga to improve their health, fitness level *and golf swing.*
Continue

Beat travel bugs

Top tips to prevent travel bugs from invading your vacation.
Continue

... and a tiny sampling of the comments.

Regarding kaylz posting: My husband is having an online affair with a 20 yr. old he met on BRladys.com, a mail order bride site. I tried confronting him but he won't admit what's he doing, because he underestimates my internet ability. I wonder if he is planning to have her come here and is just trying to hurt me enough so I leave and he still looks like the innocent victim. Anybody else have experience with these sites? Any suggestions as to what to do? — Cat

Jesse James, what about what a woman wants? What about the man who is lazy and just lays there, expecting his but not caring about yours?? It cuts both ways, baby. — PeachCa

My marriage fell apart because of several online affairs my husband had. The first time I caught him, I confronted both women he was "chatting" with and then I confronted him. He was extremely sorry. Then 4.5 years later, I caught him again . . . only this time it had been going on for over 6 months and he was falling in love with her. He was angry at me for catching him! Can you imagine?! I think that's just a knee-jerk reaction but to have the guts to do it again after being caught before is just plain stupid, in my opinion. I gave up my life and everything I knew for him. I moved to the other side of the country so he could pursue his career and I had to make friends anew. I was an 8-hour plane ride from my family . . . who was I going to turn to? I am still dealing with this problem today and I'm surprised he doesn't show a little more remorse. He's "moving on" with his life and claims he "just wants his life back." My question is, why didn't he consider that before marrying me? And what about giving me back my life? He's the one who demanded I make all the sacrifices after all.

This particular article provoked many lengthy comments, including detailed (and painful to read) accounts of shattered relationships. Clearly, many of "The New Old" are not inhibited when it comes to discussing, with great frankness, subjects that would have been taboo in previous generations.

This openness is even more dramatic when we start looking at the dating sites for certain . . . well, let's call them "sub-specialties" of the overall Boomer (and older) market.

At the start of this chapter, we talked about the cliché of "old men" pursuing sweet young things, while the dutiful wife had no choice but to tolerate the philandering — a fair description of the state of play that characterized "oldness" in previous generations. But the Boomers, as we're seeing, have put an end to that model, and now Boomer women feel quite free to pursue sex lives of their own — with Hubby, certainly, in the majority of cases, but on their own, quite happily, if necessary.

This has given rise to a "new breed" of women known as "cougars" — women who are specifically pursuing younger men primarily for sex. (I'm not saying they represent the majority of Boomer women, only that there are enough of them out there to have warranted their own label.) Not surprisingly, there are dating websites just for them.

Here's GoCougar.com.

Note how frank and matter-of-fact the language is: "Why shouldn't you date younger men?" and "You already know what you are looking for. Don't let other people decide what's right for you." Could any sentiments be more perfectly tailored to the Boomer mindset?

Here's UrbanCougar.com.

The site promises almost 19 million active members (both cougars, and the men they are looking for).

Now it doesn't matter whether or not you believe, subjectively, that these women are particularly beautiful, or that having sex with them would be as good as having sex with a 20-something Hollywood starlet. What we're talking about is the attitude, the *self*-perception, of these women. They may or may not connect through this particular online service; the important point is that they are putting themselves out there in the first place. They are utterly comfortable with wanting what they want, and still wanting it at the age they are. The handful on this particular page are in their 40s and early 50s; the attitude, as we have seen, extends to a Jane Juska, now in her 70s, and even beyond that age into the 80s (per the *New England Journal of Medicine* survey mentioned on pages 95–96).

BoomerAging means, quite simply, that sexuality — and the open and unembarrassed expression of that sexuality — doesn't disappear as you age. And this in turn has a profound effect on all other aspects of your identity as you grow older. Sexuality is a profound expression of vitality, of force, and, obviously, of engagement. BoomerAging means your sexuality doesn't have to fade away — either into the nudge-nudge-wink-wink state of "dirty old man"-hood, or into the barrenness of post-menopausal "oldness" that characterized previous generations. And this in turn means you're still a "player" in what has been, to say the least, a very important arena throughout your life.

If sex doesn't have to stop as you grow older, other things don't have to stop either.

Maybe not even *parenthood*.

Admittedly, we're talking about a tiny percentage of Boomers here. And, as with many other trends, we usually start paying attention when it happens to celebrities.

Boomer celebrity moms include:

- Cherie Blair, who had a baby at 45
- Jane Seymour, who had twins at 45
- Susan Sarandon, a baby at 46
- Iman, 44

- Cheryl Tiegs, twins at 52
- Christie Brinkley, 46
- Geena Davis, 46
- Beverly D'Angelo, twins at 49
- Holly Hunter, twins at 47

Is it just the celebs?

According to the UK's Office for National Statistics, there has been a 50% increase, compared to 10 years ago, in the number of women over 40 who are now having babies. In 1994, there were 10,241 live births to women aged 40 to 44, and 488 live births to women aged 45 and over. In 2004, these numbers jumped to 19,884 and 909 respectively.

Similar trends hold for the USA, with the rate of births to older mothers climbing steadily. In 2003, for example, there were over 1,500 births to *first-time* mothers aged 45 to 54.

The same applies, too, for Canada. In 1979, according to Statistics Canada, women aged 24 and under represented 40.7% of mothers; in 2004, this percentage had halved, to 20.6%. In 1979, birth mothers 35-plus represented 4.6% of all births; in 2004, this percentage had skyrocketed to 17.2%.

There's no question that medical science has played a huge role in this trend. Fertility treatments, coupled with better neonatal care, make it less risky for older women to bear children. But it also takes a favorable attitudinal climate: the idea that a 45-plus or 50-plus woman can not only *be* mothering a newborn, but should make active decisions to do so (and, in fact, often delay doing so at an earlier age), represents a startling change from all previous generations.

The same, of course, holds true for men. For obvious reasons, men are biologically able to become parents at much older ages than women, and there have always been some extreme examples, even decades ago (Pablo Picasso, 68; Saul Bellow, 84; Anthony Quinn, 81). But the number of "older" new fathers has now risen dramatically enough to become a reinforcement of BoomerAging, and as with women there is a strong celebrity lineup to validate the trend:

- Tony Blair was a father at 45
- London Mayor Ken Livingstone, 57

- Mick Jagger, 57
- Phil Collins, 51
- Michael Douglas, 58
- Rupert Murdoch, 72
- Rod Stewart, 60
- Paul McCartney, 61
- Eric Clapton, 59
- David Letterman, 56
- Warren Beatty, 62

Consider all the trappings of being a parent to a baby or toddler — the physical requirements, the peer groups of 20-something new parents, the need to play with and relate to an infant, the need to get involved with the play group and the school . . . it requires a mindset that goes far beyond the biological ability to reproduce. Let's go back to our by-now-familiar pairing of "oldness" and BoomerAging . . .

Isaac Kravits,
age 65

Mick Jagger,
age 63

Can you see Isaac Kravitz rolling on the floor with a toddler who was his *child?* His grandchild, sure — he used to give me great "horsey" rides and stuffed me with candy shamelessly. But sitting on a floor in a playgroup with 20-something new parents, his own child leaning up against him as the gang sings "The Wheels on the Bus"? I don't think so — do you?

But Sir Mick?

The image comes a lot more readily, doesn't it?

Being the parent of an infant and toddler imposes a need to be at least somewhat youthful in outlook. But even without this phenomenon (and the vast majority of Boomers are *not* becoming parents in their 50s) the

Boomers have retained, as we've seen, a youthful attitude — toward themselves, and toward the world around them. As a result, they are able to identify more with their children, and their children's interests and tastes, than previous generations.

A 2006 research study for Canada's BMO Financial Group reported:

"The generation gap — so prominent in the past — appears to be decreasing at a rapid rate. Almost half (49%) of 40–59-year-olds polled say they have a better relationship with their children than they had with their parents, with 60% saying their adolescent or adult children 'enjoy their company very much.' Furthermore, many respondents feel that their interests have begun to overlap with those of their children — tastes in music, for instance." In fact, the study goes on to report, 61% of Boomers said they share similar tastes in music with their children.

Perhaps I should leave the last comments to two visitors to our site, www.50plus.com. They were responding to the article, "Those sexy seniors," mentioned on page 95.

My son, now 30, says that sex is a benefit of youth and that people over 50 shouldn't be "doing it." I wonder whether he'll still feel that way, say, in 20 or so years. — Phil

Sex is all hormone driven. I am in my late 50s and my wife, junior by 8 years, helps keep the sex drive going, no idling here. Sex and love with someone close is the best. — Over 58 and still doing it

The first comment perfectly illustrates the view of sex that prevailed in a world of "oldness." The second comment perfectly illustrates the status of sex today, thanks to the influence of BoomerAging.

By now, I hope I've convinced you that the Boomers have utterly destroyed "oldness." As we've seen, there is virtually no aspect of life in which the Boomers behave the way previous generations behaved at that same age. The phenomenon of BoomerAging is pervasive, its influence is huge, and it's out there for all to see.

Logically, marketers and policy-makers would be all over this.

But as we're about to see, a ridiculously high number of them still don't

get it. In fact, what's really "old" today is the attitude of the media, marketing and policy-making communities. The implications are serious:
organizations that get what's happening will be able to take advantage of a
breathtaking range of new opportunities; organizations whose thinking is
stuck in the past will stall out or decline. So it's worth taking a brief detour
now to survey how and why the uptake has been so slow. Then we can turn
our attention to what you and your organization can do about it.

PART THREE: BUT SOME ARE STILL CLUELESS

CHAPTER 8   "They're only gonna buy one more car before they die"

In 2004, one of our advertising sales reps was calling on a media buying agency. Our rep was trying to make the case for advertising in CARP magazine, which our company publishes. It's the magazine for members of CARP — then billed as Canada's Association for the Fifty-Plus; now re-branded, thanks to Moses Znaimer's inspiration, as Canada's association for Zoomers. (With the October 2008 issue, the magazine itself is now named *Zoomer*.) With a circulation of over 175,000 households and a pass-along readership of over 700,000, it's easily the dominant print medium targeting the 50-plus market in Canada.

The media buying agency's client was a very upmarket, expensive automobile brand — and we knew that a huge percentage of its potential customers fell within our demographic group. Our sales rep was prepared to be questioned about, and to defend, a number of topics — how good was our editorial product, how did our costs compare to other magazines, etc.

But to our rep's amazement, the media buyer rejected the entire presentation before it even started: "Why should we advertise to the 50-plus? They're only gonna buy one more car before they die."

The media buyer was about 25 years old. Tops.

You might dismiss this anecdote as an aberration, an example of one breathtakingly ignorant individual and not indicative of an entire industry. (It should be pointed out, though, that this breathtakingly ignorant individual controlled several million dollars in media spending.) You might argue that the marketing industry is well aware of the size and importance of the Boomer (and now Zoomer) demographic —

how could they *not* be, given the overwhelming evidence? And haven't I myself, earlier in this book, put forward examples of companies like L'Oréal Paris and Revlon hiring celebrity spokespeople like Diane Keaton and Susan Sarandon *specifically* to target the 50-plus consumer?

Fair enough. Marketers *are* gradually "getting it" — particularly in those categories of spending (health and beauty, travel, financial services) where the buying power of the Boomers and older is most immediately apparent.

But the overall trend is still slow — slow enough, in my opinion, to be worth this entire chapter. The blunt truth is that the advertising industry is dominated by people younger — in some cases, decades younger — than Baby Boomers. As well, the industry is still the victim of myths about marketing and branding — myths that are being shattered by the Boomers themselves, right before everyone's eyes, but that still endure, for some reason, in the minds of marketers and their agencies.

As a result, there is a shocking disconnect between the *actual* influence of Boomers in the marketplace, and the perception of that influence by marketers and their ad agencies. The disconnect is shrinking, it is true, but it's still a big enough factor to constitute, in my opinion, a major problem for the marketing, advertising and media industries.

This disconnect is apparent in the experience of the Boomers themselves. In study after study, they report that they feel ignored and even marginalized by the advertising messages they see. In a poll on our own website, 80% of respondents said they didn't think Canadian marketers were interested in them, and 75% said the way they are portrayed in advertising doesn't bear any relationship to their real lives, needs, wants . . . and means.

These numbers are reinforced by much larger studies. In the USA, for example, a study by cable network TVLand indicated that almost half of Baby Boomers feel overlooked by marketers who advertise on television. Only 3% of them said they were extremely satisfied with the TV programming options available to them. And this is the generation that grew up on TV!

It's no better in the UK. A 2004 survey published by specialist marketing agency Millennium revealed that 86% of Boomers felt ignored by the marketing industry, and 70% felt patronized by advertising.

How can marketers and their ad agencies be so slow to catch on? After all, the cliché about the industry is that they'll do anything to sell their product. You'd think that, in the face of the evidence about the size and buying clout of this demographic segment, marketing to Boomers — and even to the older "seniors" — would be at the top of the priority list and not, as it is, so late, so grudging and so ineffective.

It's no accident that we got that idiotic media buyer comment, with which I started this chapter, from someone working on an automotive account. Few industries better demonstrate the disconnect between marketers and their real audience. A study conducted in 2006 by auto industry marketing research firm Auto Pacific found that only 10% of car ads were aimed at consumers over 50. But consumers in this age group purchase more cars than any other demographic segment.

"You have to look and see that the oldest boomer is hitting 60 but the youngest is 41," said George Peterson, Auto Pacific's president, in an article on Brandweek.com. But it appears that the advertising world is abandoning them in droves. The article quotes a Pontiac rep who agrees: "The Baby Boomers are not a group that will go gently into the night. ... I think we are underestimating how youthful Baby Boomers remain."

And Al Reis, a prominent marketing strategy consultant, notes it make more sense to spend ad dollars against markets in which that spending can reap results. "I wouldn't spend too much money reaching kids," he comments. "The problem fundamentally with the youth market for automobiles is that they can't afford them."

Canada represents an excellent example of just how bad the mismatch is.

Let's start with the population itself.

Here's the breakdown by age, and the projected growth rate of each group, according to Statistics Canada.

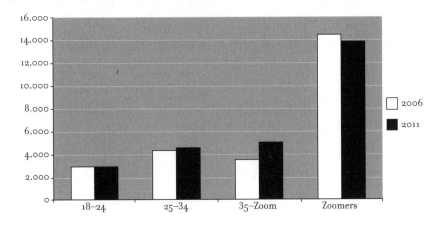

Fig. 10 — Distribution of Canadian population by age, 2006 and 2011, per Statistics Canada

As a reminder, ZoomerMedia has defined Zoomers as 44 (the youngest Boomer) on up. Here's how important that group is to the Canadian marketplace:

- There are over 14 million of them — about 42% of the entire population.
- They account for more than 50% of all consumer spending.
- They account for 82% of households with savings or securities valued at over $100,000.
- Their average household net worth is $560,484 (vs. $243,689 for households 18–43).
- They're the only age segment whose net worth increased in value between 1980 and 2001.
- They account for 68% of those who own stocks.
- They account for almost 60% of all vacation trips taken out of the country.
- They buy 80% of health care products.

· They account for 58% of all home owners.
· And best of all — thinking back to our idiot media buyer for that car manufacturer — they bought 58% of all new cars sold in Canada over the past 12 months.

With those numbers firmly in mind, let's look at the coverage of this demographic by the advertising and marketing publications in Canada. Up until 2008, there was sporadic — or no — coverage at all. To be fair, *Marketing* magazine has now planted a flag firmly in the ground, with a cover story featuring Moses Znaimer and the Zoomer phenomenon, and plans for more ongoing coverage throughout the year. But *Marketing*'s competitor, *Strategy* magazine, continues to disregard the consumers with all the money. Their special themes for 2008 include Understanding Youth (April 2008), Rising Young Media Stars (June 2008) and Nextgen Leaders (September 2008). The Zoomers, the Boomers, the 50-plus — call them what you will — get not a single mention.

Marketing and *Strategy* (and other advertising industry magazines like *Advertising Age* and *AdWeek* in the USA, and *Campaign* in the UK) are read by marketing executives, advertising agency executives, media buyers and other suppliers of marketing communications services. The companies who advertise in these magazines are, for the most part, media companies — newspapers, radio stations, TV stations, magazines, websites — who want to promote themselves as an effective venue for the spending of advertising dollars. And therein lies part of the problem: the media companies themselves have little or no interest in anything but the youth market.

Until advertisers force them from this position, that's not likely to change. To get a sense of how the media companies really feel, you can duplicate my search (November 2007) of the Time-Warner corporate website.

First, I punched in "Adults 18–34" and here's what came up:

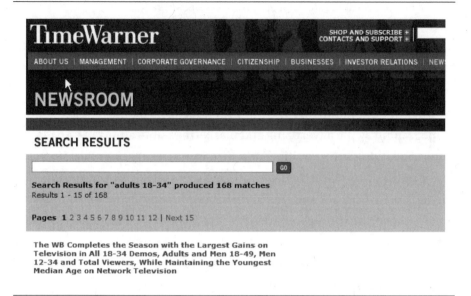

A total of 168 matches, all relating to Time-Warner's programming, its reach and its success against the 18–34 demographic. Impressive? Okay.

Now I punched in, "Adults 50+." Here's what came up:

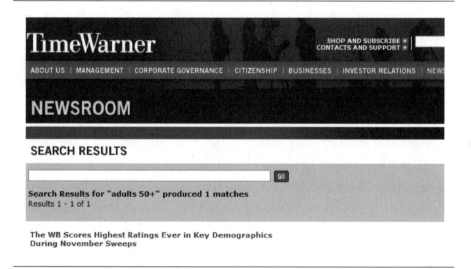

A grand total of one result.

A single story that Time-Warner was able to tell about its reach and its success with the 50-plus market.

By laying these numbers up against the actual US population, we can create a rough and ready kind of index of Time-Warner's appreciation of the marketplace.

I took the US population of 303 million (as of December 2007) and calculated the number of people who are 18–34 (72.7 million) and the number of people who are 50-plus (106.5 million). I then put that on a graph, juxtaposed with the number of references to each age group on the Time-Warner website. Here's what the graph looks like:

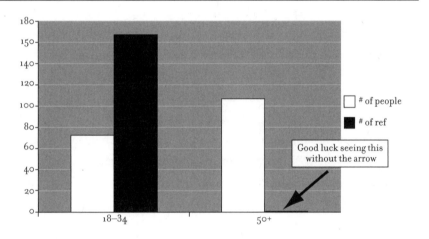

Fig. 11 — Time-Warner's Law of Demographic Importance

You can barely *see* the one reference for the 50+ age group. But the graph does allows us to set up what I am calling Time-Warner's Law of Demographic Inversion:

> The importance of a demographic segment to Time-Warner varies inversely to its importance to the marketplace.

The graph, if anything, understates the severity (and stupidity) of the law, because I based it only on the numbers of people in the respective age groups, and not on their purchasing power. The fact is that 75% of the wealth in the USA is in the hands of people who are 50 or older. Had I based the graph on this reality, the inversion would have been that much more dramatic.

Time-Warner's obtuseness is mirrored by virtually the entire media industry. As we've already noted, the TV industry is cranking out products that only 3% of Boomers find satisfying. And the newspaper industry is twisting itself into a pretzel to cater to the 18–34 market. As part of a paper produced for the Pulitzer Center (*The News, the Youth Market and the Twenty-First Century: What Do These Kids Want Anyway?*), Conor Rook vividly describes the problem:

> Newspapers across the country are experimenting with new ways to attract the 18–34-year-old demographic. Many papers have created express publications to better attract younger readers. The *Washington Post Express*, distributed free in DC subway stations, featured local, sports and entertainment news. The *Redeye*, owned by the *Chicago Tribune*, is another example of a free metro daily started in the past five years. Like the *Washington Post Express*, the *Redeye* covers mostly entertainment news. During the week of May 7, *Redeye* featured a cover story on Conan O'Brien, celebrity sightings and Michael Jackson news. Other papers like the *Post-Dispatch* have recently focused their attention on local, sports and entertainment.

Rook sees the effort as utterly futile: "The last market left is not the 18–34 demographic, but readers across the demographic chart who want and need significant in-depth news coverage."

A similar picture is painted by Susan Raitt, VP Marketing of the Canadian Newspaper Association, in an online article on "media plan makeovers":

> Advertisers tend to chase the youth market (rightly or wrongly so — that's a different article). With the target defined as the young adult, the young media planner, the young brand manager and the young creative set about their task. And let's be honest, the majority of the day-to-day work and decisions will be made by these under-30s.

Raitt's comment provides the transition we need to the question of *why* the media companies are so relentlessly chasing a market that is (a) much smaller and (b) poorer by orders of magnitude than the Boomers. Surely the media companies know the numbers. Surely they are aware of how big the various age segments are and which ones have the cash. So how to explain this continuous, and determined, heading in the opposite direction? Could it really be as simple — and as stupid — as the fact that the people making the decisions are themselves quite young, and feeding off their own misperceptions?

Yes, argues Neil Gabler, Senior Fellow at the Norman Lear Center, Annenberg School for Communications, University of Southern California. In a no-holds-barred article, "The Tyranny of 18–49: American Culture Held Hostage," Gabler is unsparing in his portrayal of the way media decisions are made, and by whom:

> It is of course no secret to any sentient being that it is a young person's world and the rest of us are just living in it. For decades now, television has appealed almost exclusively to what it considers a young audience, but so do most other media. Rock and roll, pop and hip-hop dominate the recording business . . . The teenage blockbuster has become the foundation of the American motion picture industry. Newspapers have had to renovate themselves, shortening articles and emphasizing graphics, because executives say young people won't read them otherwise. The most competitive titles in magazines are the so-called "laddie" publications aimed at young male readers. Book publishers hunt for young writers and subjects with youth appeal. Even CNN Headline News, hardly a youth destination, felt compelled to add windows and zippers to the screen reportedly as an enticement to younger viewers accustomed to sensory bombardment.

And the reason, Gabler argues, is that the people in charge are young:

> While the culture has been fixated on youth, it has also been hiring the young to service its constituents, creating a self-perpetuating system. Aging producers, aging writers, aging agents, even aging stars are increasingly marginalized because it is thought they can neither take the pulse nor race the pulse of the young. Aging talent complains that

it cannot even find representation, much less work. All of which leads to an inescapable and frightening conclusion: We live in a culture of the young, for the young and by the young, and anyone over 49 — the demographic breakpoint of old age for most television advertisers — is tossed onto the trash heap of history, all 80 million of them. In effect, these people, just under one-third of the American population, have been steadily disenfranchised by a ruthless, self-serving, myopic and ignorant dictator. That dictator is the 18 to 49 demographic cohort, and it is the single most important factor in determining what we see, hear and read.

This isn't just the complaint of an "older" person, railing against the unfairness of things. Gabler is a successful journalist, author, academic and TV producer, and very knowledgeable about how the business works. He doesn't stop here, either — he goes on to expose the idiocy of this state of affairs in business terms, as well:

. . . the only reason to get [the younger audience] is that they are worth getting, which is to say that they have money and the willingness to spend it. Conversely, the reason to spurn older viewers is that they have less money and less willingness to spend it. After all, money is money. A dollar doesn't differentiate between young and old, so advertisers should be targeting the people with the most money to spend, again assuming that they want to spend it. But here is where the appeal to youth and the rejection of those over 50 seems especially capricious. Americans over 50 years of age control 55 percent of the discretionary income in America. By contrast, the share of aggregate spending of Generation X, ages 25 to 34, was only 17.7%. The share of those geriatrics over 55 was 27.5%. In fact, according to the US Bureau of Labor Statistics, Americans between the ages of 45 and 54 spent $46,100 per household in 2000, while those under 25 spent $22,543.20. More 45- to 55-year-olds had the highest household incomes and spent more on consumer goods than any other demographic cohort. Of American households with incomes of more than

$100,000, 61% are headed by baby boomers. And this should make the broadcasters and advertisers who fixate on scarcity salivate: Households with incomes greater than $60,000 watch considerably less television than those earning below that amount. Of course, advertisers would argue that they are banking on the future and that younger consumers are a kind of investment. But once again the statistics refute this. Thirty-eight percent of Americans are now over 49, but that percentage will swell to 47 percent within 20 years. And while their numbers increase, so does their spending. Through the 1990s, Baby Boomers, aged 35 to 54, increased their share of America's aggregate spending by 6.7%, while Generation X's share actually fell a whopping 18.7%. In sum, older consumers are growing at a faster rate than younger ones, have more money to spend than younger ones, actually spend more of that money than younger ones and are increasing their spending at roughly the same rate as younger consumers. And yet they remain the lepers of television advertising.

With the argument laid out with such ruthless clarity, it seems insane that media and advertisers apparently don't get it. Can they really be that clueless?

Well, they do offer a rationale . . . of sorts. It's one of the most durable truisms of marketing: when you're younger, your brand loyalties aren't yet cast in stone. You're more liable to be influenced. So the priority is to catch a consumer when he/she is young — and advertisers are willing to pay a premium to do just that. This rationale is described well by James Surowiecki in a 2002 article in the *New Yorker* on "Ageism in Advertising":

Advertisers pay more to reach the kid because they think that once someone hits middle age he's too set in his ways to be susceptible to advertising. But at 25 he's tender. He hasn't figured out what car to drive or what beer to drink, but as soon as he does he'll be hooked. Once a Bud man, always a Bud man. As Preston Padden, the former head of ABC, said a few years ago, "Everyone agrees: brand preferences get established at an early age."

"Everyone" might agree — but the argument is completely bogus. If it were ever true at all, it's certainly become nonsense in today's world of constant new product innovation and almost limitless consumer choice. Here's Surowiecki again:

> In fact, this notion of impressionable kids and hidebound geezers is little more than a fairy tale, a Madison Avenue gloss on Hollywood's cult of youth. We're all impressionable, young and old. And, if brand preferences get established at an early age, they often get disestablished a few years later. "The least brand-loyal people are people between the ages of 35 and 54," David Poltrack, a CBS executive vice-president, said last week. A 1996 study by Information Resources found that women in that age group were more likely than younger women to abandon a favorite brand. In 1997, A. C. Nielsen found that Baby Boomers tried as many different brands of soda, beer and candy bars as 20-somethings did. Brand loyalty in general seems more and more a will o' the wisp. A few years ago, a company called the National Purchase Diary found, in a multiyear survey, that almost half the people who described themselves as loyal to a brand one year were no longer loyal to it a year later. And, according to Frederick Reichheld, of the consulting firm Bain & Company, the average American company loses half its customers every five years.

How much more evidence can we keep piling up? The numbers scream one thing; the media and marketing community does the opposite. Like Gabler, Surowiecki theorizes that one explanation may be "what economists call an internal audience problem — the people who create their ads don't look like the people who buy their products."

Surowiecki cites recent surveys showing that the average age of an ad agency Account Executive is 28. This compares to the median adult age of about 46. So the ad agencies are fielding people who are almost two decades younger than the age group that controls the marketplace. No wonder they don't "get" what's happening.

Another problem may be that ad agencies have changed their focus, and their deployment of talent, in response to the pressures and realities of their own business. David Wolfe, author of *Ageless Marketing*, expanded on this idea in an online interview on Tom Peters' website:

> Ad agencies used to be run by very bright, what I call intuitively competent people like Bill Bernbach, David Ogilvy, and Leo Burnett. The very top brains in these organizations went into client servicing. Went into figuring out the clients' marketing problems. In many cases the heads of these agencies would meet with the heads of P&G or General Motors or Chevrolet divisions or whatever, so that you had people negotiating marketing developments at the very top. You had the very best brains working on marketing.
>
> In the 1980s the whole nature of the advertising business underwent an epochal change. It started with the Saatchi brothers, when they started acquiring agencies. They started growing agencies through acquisition and merger rather than through client development. This changed the focus of agency leadership toward business development and financial matters. Over time, Martin Sorrell, who was part of that early movement with the Saatchi brothers, bought WPP, a wire baskets manufacturer, and turned it into an advertising behemoth which is now the second-largest conglomerate. It's an eight or nine billion dollar a year operation. It owns hundreds of agencies. So the top brains in WPP have not gone into client servicing. They've gone into business development through merger and acquisitions. This means that, by default, the creative output often falls to the youngest people in the agency. Because the top guys are out there trying to build business, trying to meet the numbers. In fact, someone who does work for WPP told me that throughout the WPP universe in these various companies that have been acquired, the CFO often has more power than the CEO. Because they've got to report back to London. Numbers, numbers, numbers. So creative output takes second place to numbers, and the creative output by default is falling to the younger people.

The domination of ad agencies by younger, less experienced people isn't just a North American fact. A study in England, cited in Gabler's article, found that the largest number of advertising employees were under 30, with less than 20% over 40 and only 6% over 50.

"These kids seem to shrink the world to their own horizons," says Gabler. "When a sample of young advertisers and advertising executives was asked the median age of American adults, 20% said 35.5 and half said 39. The correct answer in 1995, at the time of the survey, was 41.3 and rising rapidly."

But surely "these kids" aren't the ultimate bosses? Surely they report to vice-presidents — CEOs — *somebody* — who is older and wiser?

Gabler acknowledges that "most of the real decision-makers are not kids. They are seasoned veterans, virtually all of whom are outside the prime demographic cohort."

So why are they selling youth? Like almost everyone in their demographic cohort, but even more so given the pressures of the entertainment business, they are fighting to be relevant — fighting not to be old. It is no wonder, then, that the entire popular culture is bowing to the young. Identifying with and serving the young may be the best way for the rulers of that culture to demonstrate their own youthfulness. "There's no strong economic reason for Madison Avenue's fascination with the young audience," David Poltrack of CBS has said, missing what may be a far more powerful reason — namely that associating with the young is like professional Botox.

If true — and no one in entertainment will ever admit it — what this means is that the entire culture is tyrannized by a fiction of youth because those who command the culture are themselves tyrannized by their creation of this idealized cohort. In effect, we are beholden to their insecurities. They would have to be dragged kicking and screaming to recognize and satisfy the older viewers, listeners and readers, which is why it isn't likely to happen soon, no matter how much economic sense it makes. For people who fancy themselves as young and in the vanguard, the adjustment would be too traumatic. The rest of us have seen the future and it is older. On Madison Avenue and in Hollywood, there may be no more terrifying thought.

Which drives us back to "these kids" again.

And the sad truth is — based on everything I've read, seen, heard and experienced — they really *are* that out of touch!

AdAge.com, the website of *Advertising Age*, carried an interesting story on the generation gap between Boomerish executives and their younger colleagues. The article quoted Nancy Kramer, the 51-year-old CEO of Resource Interactive, a Columbus, Ohio, agency where nearly half of the 150 employees are under the age of 30. Kramer acknowledges her young employees don't understand the world she herself grew up in. Even limiting herself to advertising and business — never mind the wider consumer marketplace — the gap is big. "They don't understand what the '1984' commercial was for Apple, they don't understand business life before e-mail or what it was like before there was FedEx," she says.

David Swaebe, who would be the youngest Boomer (using US demographics) at 42, gives an even more dramatic example. Corporate communications director for a Massachusetts agency, he was interviewing a 20-ish job candidate. The interview took place around the Thanksgiving holiday, and Swaebe mentioned the story of Arlo Guthrie's "Alice's Restaurant." The article continues . . .

> He explained how the saga that commented on the 1960s counterculture movement took place in nearby Stockbridge, Mass., around the holiday. "The job candidate looked at me with the blankest of stares," Mr. Swaebe said. "She had no idea what I was talking about. It was a classic I'm-getting-old moment."

The article invites you to tut-tut and to hope that the ad agencies may finally be wising up. But the last sentence provides the dose of reality:

> "This is a young person's business," said Debbie Strobel, managing partner of Advertising Recruitment Specialists, who added it's rare she gets a call from an agency asking for her to hunt for a Baby Boomer. "I don't care what anyone says, agencies want the young, hot talents."

No doubt — but the evidence is strong, to say the least, that the youth-driven focus of media companies and ad agencies is not working. My complaints — and those of the authorities I have quoted in this chapter — are *not* the rumblings of "grumpy old men," not based on the bitterness of feeling unloved, but on hard numbers.

Consider, for example, the meltdown of the established media. In August 2006 . . .

- US network TV had its lowest ratings week ever (July).
- In the music business, weekly album sales set a ten-year low.
- The music-radio-listening audience had fallen 8.5% year to date, continuing a multi-decade decline.
- DVD shipments were down 4% year to date.
- Newspaper circulation continued its decades-long decline, down another 2.6% year to date.
- Magazine newsstand sales were at an all-time low, while total circulation was down marginally from the previous year.

What will it take to turn things around?

Obviously, the numbers alone won't do it. It's inconceivable that marketers and ad agencies don't know these numbers. Nobody could be that stupid and still stay in business . . . could they?

No, I think the key is that they haven't yet made the jump from the *quantitative* story to the *qualitative* story. In other words, they have completely missed the phenomenon of BoomerAging and the market power of Zoomers, of "The New Old." In their minds, the numbers simply demonstrate that there are more old people. What they don't get is that these aren't the *same* old people.

Thanks to BoomerAging, the 50-something market and the 60-something market already do not behave like people of the that age in any previous generation. And the effects are already trickling up to the 70-something market . . . and eventually, as the Boomers continue to add years, to the 80-something market and beyond.

Unless and until marketers understand the profound *qualitative* effects of BoomerAging, they will never be able effectively to reach or capitalize on this vast market.

If and when that happens, they will force change on their ad agencies — or find other means to reach that market.

If and when that happens, in turn, the media will — finally — be forced to get on board the bandwagon.

To be fair, there are signs that this is already starting. At my own company, business is booming (no pun intended) as more and more advertisers "get it." We've added new products, our circulation is growing, and our ad revenues are double the previous year. (You can get all the details at our corporate website, www.zoomermedia.ca.)

In the USA, people like Martha Stewart and Oprah have announced new magazines targeting Boomer women. More articles are appearing in the trade media (though Canada's two trade magazines aimed at the advertising industry remain locked in the past, and enthusiastically so), and there are now hundreds of websites dealing with the subject of marketing to Boomers.

In the end, of course, the numbers will win — and the overwhelming importance of this market will cause a tidal wave of hurry-before-it's-too-late action.

The question is: will it be too late for *your* organization? Do your marketing people get it? Does your agency? In later chapters, I will lay out some specific ideas and actions you should follow.

But first, let's look at the other big institution that seems absolutely clueless on this topic: you guessed it, the government.

CHAPTER 9   Boomer politics: there are none

In this chapter I am going to argue that political leaders — most of whom are Boomers themselves — absolutely do not get BoomerAging, and are hopelessly locked into obsolete notions of "oldness." I am going to show you example after example of *not* displaying even the slightest awareness of what is going on, of an ignorance or an indifference that is almost . . . well, I don't really know how to describe it . . . almost *wonderful* in its completeness. I admit that politicians represent the softest of soft targets — but boy, are they making it easy on this one.

But first — in fairness — a huge caveat. I must remind you that this is a book about *leading edge* trends, not a book that seeks to prove, statistically, that those trends describe every single solitary Boomer. Obviously, there are millions of Boomers who are *not* examples of BoomerAging, who may not have the attitudes — and, in particular, the money — to age in the ways we have been describing. And, of course, there are the rest of what I have been calling Zoomers: those who are older than the Boomers, many of whom are struggling on fixed incomes. It is entirely appropriate for politicians to want to address the needs of all these people. In no way do I argue that policies addressing "seniors" or "retirement" or "pensions" or "security" or any of the other characteristics of what we have been calling "oldness" are unimportant. To the contrary, these policies are vitally important to a caring society, and they properly belong on the political agenda.

So the problem doesn't lie with what politicians are saying or advocating; the problem lies with what they're *not* saying. The problem doesn't lie with wanting to take care of poor "old people," it lies with treating these people as the *only* manifestation of life after 45 or 50.

Politicians of all parties, on all points of the political spectrum, seem to be locked into a uniform set of beliefs and priorities:

1. Aging results in "seniors" — and no one else. There are no Boomers, Zoomers or any other types of people anywhere on the landscape.
2. "Seniors" are all retired, or about to be retired.
3. "Seniors" are helpless and, for the most part, poor.
4. "Seniors" therefore require the assistance of government programs. Taxpayers ought to be glad to pay for those programs because in so doing, they are demonstrating caring and compassion for the poor "seniors" who deserve to spend their declining years in dignity and security.
5. "Seniors" are winding down. They are essentially passive, concerned only with making it to the finish line without too much physical or financial stress.
6. "Seniors" have white hair.
7. "Seniors" are usually smiling, and are often depicted in the company of younger people whose presence in the same picture symbolizes (a) the fact that "seniors" are dependent on caregivers, (b) the need for society to be compassionate, and (c) the degree of compassion on the part of the politician or political party disseminating the information.

Since most Boomers are either not old enough, not poor enough, not frail enough or otherwise not dependent enough to qualify as a "senior," for politicians they quite literally do not exist. They are nowhere to be found in any policy statements. The influence they are already exerting on society, and on the process of aging, is — for politicians of all political stripes — utterly invisible.

We're going to look at this issue in a logical progression, under three main topics.

First, we'll take a quick tour of the major political parties in Canada, the USA and the UK. In all three cases, you're going to see an almost total absence of references to Boomers, or to any of the effects of BoomerAging.

Second, we'll survey the serious public policy issues associated with BoomerAging — issues none of the politicians are addressing.

Third, we'll talk about the politics behind all this, and how all the parties are missing out on huge opportunities. We'll show how Boomer-Aging could be a key to political power — for decades — for politicians smart enough to "get" it. (Of course that will lead you to wonder how and why they are all so blind at the moment, but that's a whole other question.)

What the politicians are — and are not — saying

Canada

I'm starting with Canada not only because that's where I live, but because, of the three countries, its politicians seem to be the *most* obtuse on this topic.

Let's begin with the ruling (as of early 2008) Conservative party. Here's an excerpt from their platform from the 2006 election — still on their website as of January, 2008. Note the final point — appointment of a Seniors Council.

Security for seniors

The Liberal track record for Canadian seniors is a sad story of unfair taxation, poor government services, and now an inexcusable policy blunder that has destroyed the retirement savings of Canadians invested in income trusts.

It is time for a government that respects those who have spent their lives raising families, saving for their retirement, and building this country.

The plan

A Conservative government will:

- Confirm its commitment to the Canada Pension Plan (CPP) and Old Age Security (OAS) as well as the Guaranteed Income Supplement (GIS) as fundamental guarantees of income security in retirement years.
- Stop the Liberal attack on retirement savings and preserve income trusts by not imposing any new taxes on them.
- Protect the integrity of the CPP investment fund to stop politicians from raiding it to balance the budget or pay for other political projects.
- Protect seniors from over-taxation by raising the pension income tax amount that is eligible for a federal tax credit from $1,000 to $2,000 per year in 2006, and to $2,500 in five years.
- Appoint a Seniors Council comprised of seniors and representatives of seniors' organizations to advise the minister responsible for seniors on issues of national importance.

Isn't that beautiful? Just in time for no one — not even those in their late 60s or 70s — to want to be called a "senior." The Council, which was created in May 2007, defines "seniors" as people 65 years of age and older.

To be fair, Senator Marjorie LeBreton, Secretary of State for Seniors and minister responsible for the Council, did touch on some topics related to BoomerAging (although of course she didn't call it that) in her inaugural remarks. She mentioned longevity, the desire of many seniors to keep working past the traditional age of retirement and future challenges to the health care system. But she also added this sentence near the very end, which shows that the Council's view of "seniors" is likely to become less and less relevant to the real world in the coming years:

"Our seniors . . . built this country, worked hard and sacrificed so the next generation could enjoy a better standard of living."

Well, okay. That might certainly describe the Boomers' parents.

But if you start defining "senior" at 65, it means that the oldest Boomers will fall under the purview of this Council as early as 2010. And by 2020, *almost half* of the "seniors" the Council is trying to serve will be Boomers. How will the Council accommodate people who hate the word "seniors"? Who are spending their kids' inheritance — and bragging about it? How smart is it to create a brand new organization in 2007, knowing that its point of view, its mandate, its very *name*, will be obsolete within less than 15 years? Or maybe they don't know. But is that possible? Could they be that out of touch?

The opposition Liberal party weighs in with the same frames of reference and the same kind of language:

As our population ages, we must also invest more in the evolving needs of our seniors. From protecting retirement savings to providing assistance for caregivers, we must enhance the quality of life for all seniors, especially those with the most limited means.

Liberals believe in a strong, just society, strong public health care, equality for all, respect for human rights and a Charter of Rights and Freedoms that protects all Canadians including all minorities from prejudice, racism, and inequality.

By investing in the lives of all Canadians, our seniors, our children, families, newcomers, and aboriginal Canadians, we can continue to build the fair and prosperous Canada we want.

"Evolving needs" at first sounds promising . . . might they actually be aware that some *new things* are happening? Nope. It turns out these needs are the same ones that have always characterized "oldness" — protect savings, help caregivers, enhance the "quality of life." Who could argue? We even have the obligatory smiling white-haired people. But there is no sign that anybody at Liberal HQ is aware of the coming influence of BoomerAging — the fact that more and more will *not* be retiring, and will emphatically *not* want to be thought of as "seniors." As with the Conservatives, it's not a matter of what is being said, but what is *not* being said.

The leftist New Democratic Party offers exactly the same point of view:

Dignity and security for seniors

Today's seniors deserve the best care we can get them and financial security in their retirement years. But after 13 years of Liberal neglect, the Conservative government is offering up more of the same—more neglect and more insecurity after a lifetime of building this country.

It's been 40 years since the last full review of income security for Canada's seniors. And in many regions, a quarter of acute-care hospital beds are filled by seniors waiting for more dignified options—because Ottawa *still* has no long-term care plan in place.

Jack Layton and the NDP are moving seniors' priorities forward in this Parliament:

- Passed a motion through Parliament directing government to work toward providing **free drug and dental coverage** for every Canadian over 65.
- Secured Parliament's approval for the NDP Seniors Charter enshrining seniors' rights to secure income, adequate housing and quality health care.
- Secured Parliament's approval for the NDP Veterans First Motion ensuring that military veterans and their families are taken care of after service.

Canada's NDP is working to get more done for seniors:

- **Better long-term care:** Work with provinces to create 50,000 long-term care spaces over five years, providing dignity and comfort to seniors who languish now in costly hospital beds.

RELATED LINKS

Government blunder shortchanged seniors: Charlton
more

NDP celebrates victory for veterans
more

NDP calls on Conservatives to support Veterans First Motion
more

NDP Veterans First Motion
more

NDP motion to protect the rights of seniors passes
more

NDP motion to include free drugs and dental for those 65 and over
more

Accessible education
LEARN MORE

Confronting poverty
LEARN MORE

Economic security for working families
LEARN MORE

Dignity for seniors
LEARN MORE

Stay Informed
SIGN UP FOR NDP's FREE E-NEWSLETTER

Email Address

Postal Code   Sign up

Once again, there are only "seniors" and what they need is dignity and security. Note the obligatory photo on the right — the smiling white-haired senior and the "caring" younger person. Boomers? Affluent seniors? People who don't want to retire — who are in fact re-inventing themselves well into their 60s and maybe even 70s? They don't exist — at least, not in the landscape of the NDP.

Now of course, there *are* tens of thousands of seniors who do need financial help, who do need better drug and dental coverage, who do deserve "financial security in their retirement years." There's certainly nothing wrong with advocating policies to help them. But as with the other two parties, there is no sign that the NDP has the faintest idea that there is any other reality but this one, as far as aging is concerned. Not a clue what's coming down the road.

United States

The Democrats currently (mid-2008) control the Congress, and are therefore in the stronger position to introduce policies that would deal with aging, Boomers, "seniors" and related issues. What's their take on the world? Have a look:

The same language as we've seen among the Canadian political parties — retirement, dignity, security. "After a life of hard work, you earn a secure retirement." Nothing wrong there, surely? But one more time — not a Boomer in sight. No mention of people who may not want to retire (ever). No vision of aging except those smiling white-haired people . . . yet again.

The Republicans are not to be outdone:

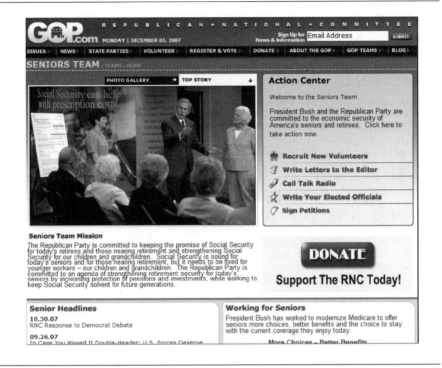

The Republicans have created what they call a "Seniors Team," and its mission is to "keep the promise of Social Security for today's retirees and those nearing retirement." The soundness (or otherwise) of Social Security is, of course, a huge topic in the USA, and we'll have much more to say about it a little later. It's certainly reasonable for the Republicans to be worrying about the issue, and to be trying to stake out a position as the "savior" of Social Security. Unfortunately, that's the beginning and the end of it — as with the other political parties that we've seen, there seems to be no recognition of the existence of Boomers, or of any of the issues that arise from BoomerAging.

And look — all that white hair again!

It's interesting, though, that one of the people with white hair is Barbara Bush, the President's mother. President Bush is himself a Boomer and could certainly be expected to understand the existence of the "sandwich generation" — Baby Boomers who are caring for 80-something or 90-something parents. But no. There is a "Seniors Team" only, and the sole issue appears to be Social Security.

The UK

Same old, same old. Here is the ruling Labour Party:

How do we ensure a dignified and secure retirement for all?

Over the last ten years pensioners have done well out of our growing economy. By combining real increases in the basic state pension with special help for the poorest pensioners, the last seven years have seen pensioners' average net incomes rise by 25 per cent – that is ten percentage points more than the rise in earnings – to around £1,500 better off a year. At the same time, we have lifted over two million of the poorest pensioners out of absolute poverty and a million out of relative poverty.

We need to make the pension system fairer, simpler and affordable for the long term. We are changing the basic state pension so that when women and men are bringing up children or caring for relatives, that contribution gets recognition in the pensions system. Almost half a million extra women currently aged between 45 and 55 will retire with a full basic state pension. We are making saving for a pension easier by giving every employee the right to a workplace pension with a contribution from their employer.

To tackle problems of saving inertia, employees will be automatically enrolled into the new low cost personal accounts scheme. We will re-link the basic state pension to average earnings. Our objective, subject to affordability and the fiscal position, is to do this in 2012 but, in any event, by the end of the next Parliament at the latest. In the long term, for this major increase in the basic state pension to be affordable we must gradually increase the state pension age by one year in each decade beginning in 2024, reaching 68 in the 2040s.

Points to consider

- What more can we do to make sure that elderly people receive all the entitlements and services they are owed?
- What more can we do to encourage young people to start saving for their pension earlier in life?

The language is absolutely interchangeable with that of Canada's Conservative, Liberal and New Democratic parties, or with the Republicans and Democrats in the USA. "Dignified and secure retirement." "Elderly people" who need to receive "the entitlements and services they are owed." All good and important, to be sure. But no sign that aging means anything other than poor and dependent "elderly."

Here are the Liberal Democrats:

One more time: pensions and benefits, retirement, old people with white hair. No sign of any Boomers on the landscape.

It is only when we turn to the Conservatives that we can find the actual word "Boomer" within a reasonable number of clicks. (I went as deep as 15 clicks on all the other party websites and still found no trace of Boomers.) Not on the official policy part of the website, mind you:

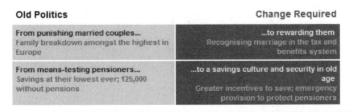

Here it's just more of the same. Pensioners, savings, security. But there is also a lengthy reference to Boomers in a speech to the Conservatives' 2006 conference, by Shadow Secretary of State for Education and Skills David Willetts.

The Challenge to the Baby Boomers

Let me ask a simple question. Do you, the people in this audience, middle-aged and some perhaps a bit older than that, believe that you have enjoyed opportunities and prosperity greater than your parents did? I believe that for most of us the answer is yes. But are you confident that your children or grandchildren will similarly enjoy better lives, more secure and more prosperous than ours? I am not so sure about that. Many people fear that somehow we are not passing on to the next generation opportunities as great as we have enjoyed ourselves. It is a fundamental obligation that each generation has to try to pass on something a bit better for the next generation.

Here at last is someone who at least acknowledges the existence of the topic!

Mr. Willetts, in fact, seems well informed (by orders of magnitude, compared to the other politicians) about some of the issues created by, and affecting, Baby Boomers. A Boomer himself (born in 1956), a veteran policy analyst, author, expert on pensions and benefits, and member of the Global Aging Commission, he obviously has a handle on what is going on.

The speech, mind you, is something of a scold-cum-apology. "Do you remember Tony Benn saying that he wanted to achieve a fundamental shift of power and wealth to working people?" Willetts asks. "Well, what we have done is instead to deliver a fundamental shift of power and wealth to the Baby Boom generation, roughly the people born between 1945 and 1970. There are so many of us that we have created a world that reflects our culture and is shaped around our economic interests. We haven't quite been selfish but we have been more than lucky."

Lucky . . . and not very kind to those who follow.

"We Baby Boomers haven't just bought our houses cheap and written off the borrowings with high inflation. We've then pulled up the ladder behind us by restricting the supply of housing as well, further pushing up prices. So now the next generation face high house prices and are finding it incredibly difficult to get started on the ladder at all."

The thrust of the speech is an attack on debt, and Willetts delivers an attack on then-Chancellor of the Exchequer and now-PM Gordon Brown with language that reveals a familiarity with BoomerAging: " . . . because of the way that Gordon Brown has been running the public finances we have been building up an enormous amount of debt. . . . These debts are going to have to be paid out of the next generations' incomes. The Chancellor should have a bumper sticker on his Ministerial car reading, 'Spending the Kids' Inheritance.'"

He goes on to amplify what the Boomers have wrought in language that would do credit to Boomer-hater Paul Begala: "A young person could be forgiven for seeing Britain's economics and political structure as nothing less than a conspiracy by the Baby Boomers in our own interests. It goes way beyond economics. We shape the culture as well to remind the Baby Boomers of when they were growing up. That's why the Mini has just been re-launched, the Rolling Stones still go on tour, and Twiggy is modeling again."

It's not my purpose to go into the specifics of Willetts' position, particularly the financial details (although it's worth noting that as I write this, in mid-2008, housing prices have started to come down in the UK in the wave of the USA's subprime mortgage bloodbath — so perhaps Willetts was taking on a little too much generational guilt). The important thing is that he obviously sees what is happening and shows some understanding of its impact. He's the sole politician I was able to find — short of clicking into tens upon tens of links and sub-links — who displayed any such awareness at all. Willetts aside, all the political parties share the same vision of what aging means. (Or at least, they communicate only that vision.)

Here is that vision. To have a little fun, see if you can match the photo with the party. I've supplied one correct answer to get you started.

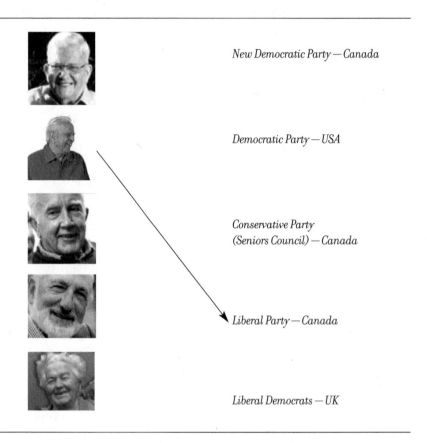

They all blend together, don't they?

Now here we have right-wing, centrist, left-wing — all areas of the political spectrum are represented. We have political parties who believe in strong, activist governments that should be busy-busy-busy adjusting the way society operates; we have parties who believe in lesser degrees of government involvement.

Yet they all display essentially *the same view of aging*: that aging produces only one set of circumstances worthy of note (much less action); namely, the presence of impoverished retirees who are almost entirely dependent on the government to enable them to have a secure, dignified wind-down of their lives. If there are other people engaged in the aging process whose circumstances do *not* fit this stereotype, their presence is not even mentioned, much less dealt with.

If I were to stop here, you might say I was simply a complainer. Yes, it is striking almost to the point of hilarity to see how obtuse all the politicians appear to be; yes, it is fun to match the white-haired photos against the party names; yes, Cravit certainly found more than a handful of Internet screen grabs to make politicians look dumb.

But so what? We already know politicians are dumb. You're being too sensitive, Cravit. So what if they either don't know about, or are indifferent toward, Boomers and BoomerAging? Now that you've had your fun ridiculing them, get over it.

That would be a perfectly justifiable reaction if all I were doing was offering my rant and then leaving it at that.

But in fact, there are very substantial public policy issues tied up with BoomerAging and the emergence of the New Old. The Boomers' destruction and re-invention of the entire process of aging is going to have profound effects on our society — is in fact already starting to have those effects. There are time bombs ticking away, and it is mind-boggling that all major political parties seem unaware of them. Instead, they are locked into a thought process, a construct, that is obsolete; they share a view of aging that is simplistic, one-dimensional, and ultimately dangerous in its neglect of serious challenges to public welfare.

To be fair, as I have already acknowledged, the one aspect that they *are* focusing on — "seniors" and poverty or the threat of poverty — is certainly a crucial topic that is entirely worthy of attention and policy debate. The combination of longer life spans and fixed incomes confronts millions of people with serious risks, and it is right and proper that politicians declare their awareness of those risks and their intentions to deal with them.

BoomerAging, powerful and pervasive as it is, does not eliminate "oldness" and replace it with a new model overnight; it coexists with previous models, and those millions of people still living according to those earlier models must be helped as much as possible.

That said, BoomerAging presents a whole new set of challenges to public policy. I am going to examine just one of the biggest: health care. I should emphasize that it is *not* my mandate to comment on what political philosophy (right-wing, left-wing, interventionist, laissez-faire) is best suited to deal with these challenges, or what political party or set of policies should be supported. (In any case, as we have seen, there are virtually no points of view on offer from the politicians right now.) My only purpose is to show the kind of upheaval that is coming — which makes the politicians' ignorance or lack of interest all the more remarkable.

It's understandable that health care would be a major concern for Boomers. As we've seen in a previous chapter, they need to be in good health in order to maintain the level of engagement and activity that BoomerAging inspires, and they are also highly motivated to seek out and use new medical breakthroughs to extend their life span even more. At the same time, a significant number of them are caring for elderly parents, so they have direct exposure to the health care delivery systems of today.

It's a powerful combination of forces: an involved, affluent segment of the population, highly engaged in the topic and constantly on the prowl for new and better answers, and numerous enough to exert a significant influence.

The "net net" is that the Boomers will destroy and rebuild health care as we know it. Since there are important differences in the existing systems of the three countries we've been following throughout this book — Canada, the USA and the UK — we have to start by looking at each country individually. Then we can make some wider observations about the future impact of BoomerAging on health care.

Canada

Of the three countries, Canada has the most curious health care model. Not only is there state-run health care, available for free, but the system more or less makes any private health care illegal for services offered by the state. Since health care is administered by the provinces, there is considerable variation in this state of affairs, with some provinces (for example, Quebec and British Columbia) showing much more tolerance for private health care than others (for example, Ontario). But the prevailing policy point of view is that Canada's system represents not only a determination to make medical care available to everyone, regardless of ability to pay, but also to prevent anyone from having access to the system — or to any alternative system — on more favorable terms (i.e., faster) than anyone else. The enemy is "two-tier" health care, often described by politicians as "US-style" health care. The goal is not only to deliver good quality health care, but to prevent anyone from purchasing, with their own money, even better quality health care.

This model is shared by only two other countries in the world — Cuba and North Korea — yet it has been defended passionately by politicians of all three major political parties:

- Conservative Prime Minister Brian Mulroney called medicare "a sacred trust."
- Liberal Prime Minister Paul Martin said (after a Supreme Court ruling struck down Quebec's ban on private health insurance), "We're not going to have a two-tier health care system." (Interestingly, his own physician, Sheldon Elman, was the founder and CEO of the Medisys Health Group, which operates a chain of private MRI clinics.)
- Current Prime Minister (as of July 2008) Stephen Harper has twisted himself into a pretzel to avoid seeming to be openly critical of the existing system (while tolerating, and some think actively supporting, experimentation with alternative models).
- The left-wing New Democratic Party, not surprisingly, has been consistent — and strident — in its defense of the current system. "Our single-payer system means this," said NDP leader Jack Layton in a 2005 speech, "when you go for medically necessary health care, the doctor sends the bill to the government, instead of to you."

The trouble with all this rhetoric is that it flies in the face of reality. The politicians are not only defending a model that cannot survive, but they are describing a health care system that no longer, in fact, exists.

Health care costs are eating up government budgets. Public sector spending on health care represents about 70% of all health care spending in Canada, and these costs have been rising at a faster rate than the rate of increase in government revenues.

In a paper published in 2007, Brett Skinner, Director of Health, Pharmaceutical and Insurance Policy Research at The Fraser Institute, a conservative think tank, wrote, "Government health spending in six of the ten provinces is on pace to consume more than half of total revenues by the year 2020, two thirds by the year 2035, and all of provincial revenue by 2050." This doomsday scenario is supported by a 2006 estimate by British Columbia Finance Minister Carole Taylor that if health care spending in that province continued at recent annual rates, it would account for 71% of the entire provincial budget by 2017.

Faced with these numbers, governments are scrambling wildly. In some provinces, services are cut or delisted. In Ontario, for example, there is already two-tier health — those who can pay privately, those who can't — for physio-therapy, occupational therapy, psychology and routine eyesight checkups.

But the biggie is prescription drugs. In 1975, spending on prescription drugs represented 8.8% of all health care spending in Canada; in 2007, this category represented 16.8%. The huge increase is partly due to the growing importance of prescription drugs, as the continuing pace of scientific research and discovery produces more powerful drug therapies, and partly due to the aging of the population and the resulting need for drugs to deal with chronic conditions. Pre-scription drug spending is now the second-biggest category of health care spending, and rising. Hospitals, the largest category, account for 28.4%, but this is down from 44.7% in 1975 and 31.5% in 1997. Spending on doctors is actually the *third*-highest category, at 13.4%, a figure that has been relatively stable over the past 10 years or so.

The mix is critically important, because prescription drugs are not part of Canada's medicare system. Private insurance is the norm, and government plans that do exist are run by the provinces, primarily for "senior citizens" 65 years of age and older. And those provincial plans represent a checkerboard of coverage, varying wildly from jurisdiction to jurisdiction, with drugs that are covered in Province A not necessarily covered in Province B. Of 24 of the newest and most powerful intra-venous cancer drugs, for example, in 2007 British Columbia's drug plan covered 20 while Ontario's drug plan covered only 4.

There is also a growing pressure on governments to cut wait times, and the federal government introduced a wait time guarantee program — virtually useless, since it was up to each province to actually deliver on the guarantee. The progress has been, at best, uneven.

The wait time problem is so acute that in 2005 the Canadian Supreme Court struck down a Quebec prohibition on private health insurance, basing its reasoning on the existence of long waiting lists for health services. In the case, *Chaoulli v. Quebec*, private citizen George Zeliotis and physician Jacques Chaoulli argued that banning private health insurance would contravene the Quebec Charter of Human Rights and Freedoms (right to life, right to security of person) because the monopoly government health service was unable to deliver treatment on a timely basis. Zeliotis had been placed on a long waiting list for orthopedic surgery, while Chaoulli had been denied a license to open a private hospital. "The delays that are the necessary result of waiting lists increase the patient's risk of mortality or the risk that his or her injuries will become irreparable," the Court ruled. "The evidence also shows that many patients on non-urgent waiting lists are in pain and cannot fully enjoy any real quality of life. The right to life and to personal inviolability is therefore affected by waiting times."

Bolstered by this ruling, private alternatives to the state health care monopoly have been steadily increasing. The newly elected president of the Canadian Medical Association, Dr. Brian Day, is the founder of the Cambie Surgery Centre, a private orthopedic surgery facility in British Columbia, and an outspoken advocate of a public/private system. He is only one of a growing number of voices who are pointing out the "Emperor's new clothes" nature of Canada's health care policy — politicians continuing to pretend that the model can work and that the fight against "two-tier" health care represents some kind of higher moral calling (and an important part of the Canadian identity), while in the real world everyone knows the system is a mess and that if you get sick, it's simple common sense to try to jump the queue or go the USA or do whatever you have to do to get prompt treatment.

A recent article on our flagship site, www.50plus.com, detailed the growing privatization of the Canadian health care system, placing into sharp relief the increasingly Alice-in-Wonderland viewpoints of most Canadian politicians.

The article generated thousands of clicks within days, and it's interesting to note some of the reader comments that were posted online:

There's no denying that we already have had, for many years, a two-tiered system . . . we have the brain to do it, just not the guts to look outside the box when it comes to health care.

Right on! Let's get our head out of the sand and do what is necessary. The number of countries that have tried a state-run approach to health care for its citizens and failed is legion.

So many of us have seen first-hand what you describe. Pouring more money would just add one more level of incompetence.

I get so sick and tired about this private and/or public debate. If a private firm cannot compete it goes broke; if the public plan can't compete, it should go broke.

Bravo! You are sooooooooooooo right. Now, how we make the puppet government of this country listen and make the appropriate changes.

This is an excellent review of the current health care debate and includes an objective calm assessment of the situation. The question is and remains — if you are in pain or need help, do you really care how you get it? It is true that the political niceties of public or private medical pale the longer it takes to get the qualified professional service help you need to relieve your health pain.

To be fair, there were also a number of spirited defenses of the current model. The important point is that the debate is taking place at all — and so vociferously — and in the continued absence of very much discussion from the politicians. "Canadians are ahead of their politicians on health care," wrote *National Post* columnist Jonathan Kay in a September 2007 column. "Ordinary people are ready for real reform — it's the politicians who are mired in Trudeau-era dogmas." Kay quotes Dr. Albert Schumacher, former president of both the Canadian and Ontario medical associations: "The politicians won't touch it with a 10-foot pole."

It goes beyond my level of competence to determine why Canada's politicians have (willingly, it seems) locked themselves into such a foolish construct. Given the prevalence of public/private hybrids throughout Europe, for example, it would have been easy for them to be simultaneously in favour of a robust public health care system and at least making it *legal*, for heaven's sake, for citizens to spend their own dollars, if they so choose, on private alternatives. We are, after all, talking about matters of life and death. But for some unfathomable reason, politicians of all three political parties chose to box themselves into a corner — a corner that already looks undefendable and will become ever more so as the tidal wave of Boomer-Aging really starts to bite.

Because make no mistake — it will be the Boomers who will finish off Canada's model. They won't tolerate the long waiting times for care for their own parents. They will tolerate it even less for themselves.

As we saw in a previous chapter, they are already going online, in droves, to look for medical services and products. We have seen brand-name knees, searchable databases of discount heart surgery suppliers, medical tourism — the Boomers are *active shoppers* for better health and for longevity. The notion that they will sit passively by, willingly taking a bullet as far as their own health and well-being is concerned for the sake of some misguided view of Canadian identity that depends on Canada *not* doing whatever America is doing — which seems to be precisely the notion held by most Canadian politicians — will prove to be as delusional as the politicians' belief in the efficacy of the model itself. Within ten years, some politician will have the guts to puncture the balloon — and he or she will reap an avalanche of benefit at the polls (more on this below). What is certain is that the Boomers, whose numbers and whose needs are already beginning to burden the creaky system even more, will have no compunction about sweeping it aside in the service of their own health and wellness needs.

A good indicator of what's coming is Timely Medical Alternatives, a Vancouver-based service that promotes itself quite frankly as helping Canadian clients jump the queue:

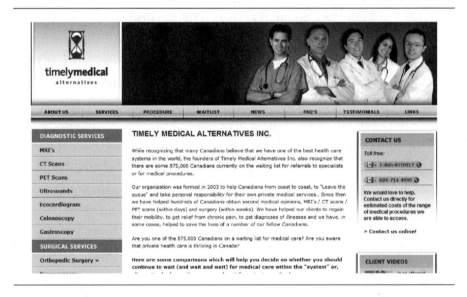

"Our organization was formed in 2003," the website notes, "to help Canadians from coast to coast, to 'leave the queue' and take personal responsibility for their own private medical services." While Boomers are of course not the only people who might share this kind of attitude, the statement is certainly an excellent illustration of the Boomer mindset — independence, distrust of institutions, determination to take charge in order to get what one needs.

The website also reflects consumer-friendly marketing, with a specific "compare-before-you-buy" chart:

Here are some comparisons which will help you decide on whether you should continue to wait (and wait and wait) for medical care within the "system" or, alternatively, leave the queue and wait for private medical care:

Procedure	Wait Times in Public System*	Private-pay Wait Times for Clients of TMA**
Knee Replacement	Up to 2 years	3 Weeks
Gall Bladder Removal	Up to 3 years	3 Weeks
Angiograms	Up to 6 months	24 Hours
Angioplasty	Up to 12 months	48 Hours
Cardiac Bypass	Up to 12 months	48 Hours
Arthroscopic Shoulder Surgery	Up to 2 years	3 Weeks
Spinal Disectomy	Up to 3 year	3 Weeks
MRI	Up to 6 months	2 Days
CT Scans	Up to 4 months	2 Days
Ultrasound	Up to 4 months	2 Days
Weight loss Surgery	Up to 5 years	2 Months

As we have already seen in an earlier chapter, the Internet has become the primary medium for health-related research, enabling "patients" to become "shoppers." It is easy to predict a future in which the databases will become even more extensive, and "shoppers for health" will quickly and conveniently be able to book appointments around the world online. The idea that Canada's rigid system could survive in such a world is laughable. The Boomers will be the first patients to become truly worldwide comparison shoppers, moving quickly from one set of suppliers to another, seeking the most up-to-date solutions, the best value, the most convenience. Health care will become increasingly privatized, not as a result of philosophical changes in top-down policy, but as a result of the independent action of millions of affluent, mobile, demanding individuals who will not sit still for slow, costly and inflexible solutions where their own health and well-being is concerned.

That doesn't mean, of course, that they will endorse any and all private care systems. This is going to be about *outcomes*, not about political ideology. The very demanding Boomers will apply the same ruthless examination of costs and results to the mostly for-profit US system as they do to the Canadian one. And they are already finding plenty to criticize.

USA

If Canada's Soviet-style approach to health care is doomed, it doesn't mean the privately based USA system is a winner, either.

The USA, without a state-run medical system like Canada or the UK, actually spends more on health care. On a per capita basis, total health expenditures in the USA were $6,711 in 2003, compared to $2,998 for Canada and $2,317 for the UK (all figures in US$). This represented 15.2% of GDP — up from 8.8% in 1980 — a larger increase than in any other high-income country. (The Canadian number in 2003 was 9.9% of GDP, while the UK spent 7.8% of GDP.)

The American system is beset by the same demographic challenges as Canada and the UK, and some additional problems — sky-high non-medical administrative costs due to a proliferation of systems and insurers, inconsistent standards of insurability and over 40 million people with no insurance at all. There have been horror stories of people who have had to mortgage their homes to pay for expensive surgery, or go without food to pay for lifesaving prescription drugs. As I write this (March 2008), health care has become a major domestic policy issue in both the Presidential and Congressional campaigns for 2008. "In the wealthiest, most powerful nation on earth," say the Democrats on their campaign website, "no one should have to choose between taking their child to a doctor and paying the rent. Democrats are committed to making sure every single American has access to affordable, effective health care coverage." The Republicans remain committed to private insurance, but concede it has to be more affordable so that more people are covered: "Americans are fortunate to have the most advanced and innovative health care system in the world," their website declares. "The President's plan will make private health insurance more affordable and increase the number of Americans with health insurance. The plan will also help our Nation move away from reliance on government-run health care and toward a system in which Americans have better access to basic, affordable private insurance, and increased ownership of their medical decisions."

Almost everyone agrees the US system has serious problems. For all the anecdotes about Canadian Boomers going to the USA to avoid Canada's horrendous wait times, when it comes to health care "the grass is greener" syndrome apparently works the other way, too. For example, a 2004 opinion poll by Harris Interactive revealed that, by a margin of 49% to 34%, more Americans felt positive about the Canadian health care system than about their own.

Both systems now have to cope with the aging of the population and, in particular, the flood of Boomers. The USA is halfway along a process that will see the over-65 population *triple* between 1980 and 2030. Commenting on a 2007 report prepared for the American Hospital Association on the coming impact of Boomers, association president Rich Umbdenstock spoke of a "tidal wave" of health needs. "Boomers are just the beginning," he said. "The good news is more of us will be active and enjoying our later years. But to meet the health challenges that come with that, we will need a greater focus on wellness and prevention, new approaches to care delivery, and a new look at the American health care system."

Certainly the challenges will be formidable. The AHA report notes that more than 37 million Baby Boomers — that's six out of ten — will be managing more than one chronic condition by 2030. One out of four, or 14 million, will be living with diabetes. Half will be living with arthritis — a number that reaches 26 million by 2020. Another 21 million — more than one out of three — will be considered obese.

As a consequence, demand for services will skyrocket. By 2020, the Boomers will account for 40% of all office visits to physicians — and projections show there's no way the number of physicians (not to mention nurses or other primary care providers) will keep up with the demand. There will be no slowdown, though, in the pace of medical advances, and these will be eagerly sought by Boomers.

There is no sign of any of these issues in the policy deliberations of either major political party.

Yet these challenges could "overwhelm American public policy," argue Richard D. Lamm, a former governor of Colorado, a 1996 US presidential candidate (Reform Party) and director of the Center for Public Policy and Contemporary Issues at the University of Denver, and Robert H. Blank, a research scholar at New College of Florida, in a 2005 article in the *Futurist* magazine. "The US retirement system is now actuarially unsustainable," they point out, "and health care expenditures in the nation have grown over the past 40 years at about two and one-half times the rate of inflation, now consuming more than 15% of GDP. Thoughtful people are coming to realize that, given society's seemingly endless production of new miracle treatments, the efforts expended to maintain our own aging bodies can bankrupt our children and our grandchildren."

Failure to act soon, they maintain, could force "truly draconian" decisions. They warn: "Age could well be as divisive in the next 40 years as race and sex have been for the last." Already there is a critical imbalance — while the "elderly" account for 13% of the population, they receive more than 60% of all federal social spending. "It is not a workable nation-building strategy to spend significantly more on the last generation than we do on the next generation. We must re-think many of our basic public policy assumptions, because the status quo in health care and retirement spending is no longer an option."

The article details the problem vividly:

We simply have invented and discovered more things to do to our bodies than our aging society can afford. We now are on the threshold of the bionic body, where medicine can have some positive impact on practically every organ. Modern medicine has outrun the ability of any nation, even a rich nation, to pay for everything beneficial to everyone within its borders. We have created a Faustian bargain, where our aging bodies can and will divert resources that our children and grandchildren need for their own families and that public policy needs for other important social goods.

Lamm and Blank eventually argue for a system that rations health care for the widest possible good: "We need a method of assessing health needs that looks not at individuals, but at the broader health producing possibilities. Public policy must quantify 'need' cumulatively and relate that need to the real world of affordable/sustainable resources. In short, we need a public policy that values universal health care coverage."

This is not a book about health care policy, so I don't propose to go into the details of what they have in mind. Our interest is in linking the situation to the wider topic of Boomers and BoomerAging, and in this context it is fair to point out that the proposed approach flies in the face of what the Boomers are going to want. Lamm and Blank concede as much when they note, "To some degree, a two-level health care system is inevitable since individuals have the right to spend their own money as they see fit. Thus, whatever level of health care that government or health plans may provide, some patients may choose to supplement that benefit by spending their own funds."

Exactly.

A big fan of that "spending their own funds" idea is Harvard Business School Professor Regina Herzlinger, arguably America's most prominent advocate of market-driven health care. "The US health care system is in the midst of a ferocious war," she writes in her latest book, *Who Killed Health Care?* "Four armies are battling to gain control: the health insurer, hospitals, government and doctors. Yet you and I, the people who use the health system and who pay for all of it, are not even combatants." Herzlinger believes that giving consumers more power would drive down costs, increase efficiencies and result in better health care for more people. Long a voice in the wilderness, her views are gradually gaining support as policy-makers struggle to cope with the challenging dynamics. What's interesting — in our particular context in this book — is that she sees increased demand (and consumer power) as a force for profound change. And the leading edge of that demand will be the Baby Boomers, whom she describes as "the most manipulative, self-seeking and effective generation that this country has ever seen." If she's right, the combination of increased need, increasing numbers and the "I want what I want" mindset will make Boomers the driving force behind health care reform. Boomers will not willingly allow anything to stand in the way of the kind of health services they need in order to fulfill the process of BoomerAging.

UK

The UK has a hybrid system: a state-run public health service (National Health Service, or NHS) coexisting with private health care. The UK faces the same demographic challenges as Canada and the USA, and the Baby Boomer generation is, as we have seen, as influential in its size and economic clout.

The National Health Service was introduced in 1948, so it has been a defining feature of all British Boomers' lives. The NHS has apparently recognized the coming challenges; in 2000 it introduced a plan for reform "to give the people of Britain a health service fit for the 21st century: a health service designed around the patient." The NHS was frank in admitting its past shortcomings: "The NHS is a 1940s system operating in the 21st century world. It has: a lack of national standards, old-fashioned demarcations between staff and barriers between services, a lack of clear incentives and levers to improve performance, and over-centralization and disempowered patients."

To remedy this underperformance, the plan called for a 50% increase in cash allocated to the NHS, an increase in the number of health care facilities and improvements to existing facilities, modern IT systems and significant investments in medical training so as to increase the number of health care professionals. The plan also called for tougher national standards, but more decentralized implementation: "There will be a new relationship between the Department of Health and the NHS to enshrine the trust that patients have in front-line staff." The plan also called for increased usage of private providers of health care "to enable the NHS to make better use of facilities in private hospitals" although "NHS care will remain free at the point of delivery — whoever provides it." (The last point has been hotly debated in Canada, with most politicians treating as heresy the notion that publicly funded health care can be provided by privately owned services.)

The NHS has also conducted considerable research in health issues as they affect Boomers and has developed some interesting educational models aimed at reducing the health care impact of aging by encouraging healthier lifestyles at mid-life — in effect, working backward to reduce problems in one's 70s or 80s by influencing wellness and prevention behavior in one's 50s and 60s.

On balance, one would have to say that — on paper, at least — the British system seems far more in tune with what is really going on out there, and what challenges are in the pipeline, than either the Canadian or US systems.

So what has been the reaction?

British Boomers are highly skeptical of government and big institutions. The 2004 Demos Research study, "Eternal Youths: How the Baby Boomers Are Having Their Time Again," which I have cited in Chapter 6, makes that clear: "British Baby Boomers have higher expectations of service provision than both younger and older generations, and . . . are more reluctant to put their trust in public service managers. More generally, most of our Boomer interviewees were extremely loath to put their trust in government or other institutions." The report goes on to say: "The uphill struggle which government faces in winning the trust of Baby Boomers was amply demonstrated when our Baby Boomer interviewees were asked to evaluate schemes which might improve their quality of life. Many saw the schemes as a simple example of cost-cutting by automation and routinisation."

This mindset certainly applies to the NHS and health care. "Eternal Youths" quotes a 2002 study by the MORI Social Research Institute, revealing that only 5% of Baby Boomers thought the NHS would improve — compared to 18% of the under-34s and 19% of the over-55s. "But the Baby Boomers are not only disillusioned by services," the "Eternal Youths" report goes on to say, "they are also more assertive than any previous generation in demanding what they take to be their rights. Their assertiveness will, over the next decade, have profound implications for how many of our public services are organized. [A report on the future of NHS funding] has already argued that 'it is likely that future older people will be increasingly intolerant of any differential access to services. They are likely to be more demanding of the health service, thanks to greater awareness of health and available interventions.'"

Sound familiar?

Some of this unhappiness is already beginning to manifest itself on the political scene. The *Observer* carried an article in October 2005, by Gaby Hinsliff, its political editor, suggesting that "the aging of Britain, as the 'Baby Boomer' generation hits retirement, could cost Labour 10 seats at the next election." The article deals with a report from Age Concern, a research and social policy organization, that included evidence of a lot of dissatisfaction with the NHS. "As Baby Boomers feel the first twinges of impending mortality, concern over the NHS is also rising, with a common perception that 'money has been wasted and not led to better services.'"

Health care: summary

Our quick survey of Canada, the USA and the UK illustrates how out of touch political leaders are with the coming influence of Boomers and Boomer-Aging. While they may certainly be aware of the raw numbers — the rising demand, the dollar cost to the health care system — and while some of them show signs of thinking about the impact on current models, there's almost no sign of any realization of just how profound and pervasive the influence of BoomerAging will be on health care.

Of course, not all Baby Boomers are aging in the same way: it's a point I have made before, and it is important to repeat it in this context. Health care systems will evolve and not be transformed overnight; there will be tens of millions of people who, as they age, will behave in exactly the same way and have exactly the same needs as "old people" of previous generations. Their burden on the system will be mathematical, and not behavioral — there will simply be so many more of them that the dollar costs will skyrocket. Rigid systems like Canada's will not be able to cope; change will be driven by dollar necessity, not by any sudden wisdom of the tone-deaf politicians.

But in the midst of all this, there will be a critical mass of Boomers who *are* the drivers of BoomerAging, and who will not behave the way any previous generation has. And there will be enough of them to constitute a permanent leading-edge irritant to the system, a force that cannot be contained by any of the "top-down" models. In an important sense, public health care policy will be an irrelevancy to them — they will work both within, and around, whatever system is in place, so as to net out with what-ever they need. They will be the vanguard that creates the consumer-driven health care model that Regina Herzlinger advocates, and they will create it not because it is idealistically or philosophically superior to what is on offer now, but because their demands will trump everything.

Their presence, and their influence, will stand public policy on its head. Public policy in health care is predicated on a search for the best system; it is a "top-down" design problem, ruled by a combination of ideology, expertise and (optimistically) learning from experience. (And, to be fair, since the government doles out the money, it has the right to design the money-spending structure.) BoomerAging, however, makes "the system" just one more feature of the "me-first" landscape — to be dealt with and used if it is to one's advantage to do so; to be by-passed if it is not.

BoomerAging will create a powerful cohort of freelancers, of independent health care shoppers, empowered by the Internet to be able to search quickly and conveniently for the best combination of service and price, and with the means and the mobility to go wherever they have to (or to have the services come to them). BoomerAging will create a worldwide market for health care, freeing "consumers" from the restrictions of their particular national systems and enabling cross-border "shopping" for whatever is needed. Medical tourism, now in its infancy, will become an increasingly important source of revenues for countries, like India, that can combine state-of-the-art technology with cost advantages. A whole new level of brokers, packagers and other service providers will be able to aggregate health services and products and serve them up to aging (and affluent) Boomers on a global basis.

It will be argued that this "new world" that I envision will be very unfair. Private providers will be able to cherry-pick the wealthiest "consumers," leaving the national health care systems stuck with "patients" who are older, sicker and poorer. This is likely to be true. But remember — I am not being an advocate here, I am simply describing the inevitable impact of BoomerAging on health care.

Other issues

BoomerAging will sweep away most of the policy assumptions and institutional constructs that politicians *think* still matter — yet, as we have seen, they display little interest. I have focused on health care because it provides one of the most vivid examples of this indifference — all the more remarkable since it is a topic of such critical importance. But there are other time bombs ticking away; two, in particular, will dramatically reshape society as we know it. And once again, politicians appear to be missing in action.

The table on the next pages summarizes some of the key issues, the challenges they throw at current assumptions and the policy implications for the future (if only the political leaders would start paying attention).

Table 6 — Selected BoomerAging issues politicians seem unaware of

Topic	Key issues	Government departments/ policy areas affected
Employment — Boomers staying	Boomers can't afford to retire; want to stay in the workforce; government must encourage this or be faced with crippling pension/welfare problems	– Pensions – Job training and re-training – Mandatory retirement laws – Taxation – Small business loans
Employment — Boomers retiring	Huge number of Boomers will, in fact, retire; this will leave critical labor shortages and serious loss of knowledge base = lower productivity	– Education and training – Innovative new apprenticeship models in which Boomers mentor young workers – Flexible work-from-home consulting – Labor policies – Union policies
Housing	Boomers have no interest in going into nursing homes, even at "end of life" stage; will demand, invent innovative new forms of housing to combine independent living with assisted living	– Housing policies – Mortgages – Tax deductibility – Zoning and transportation – Integrated tech/health solutions – Caregiving (resources, training, tax policies) – Re-invention of institutional care for when it finally becomes unavoidable
Education	Boomers will represent huge market for continuing education from college degrees to non-credit "learning for its own sake" to job skills; will become major new source of revenue for colleges, especially if programs can be delivered through remote (Internet) learning	– Education – Educational financing – Teacher training (whole new specialty in teacher education will be how to teach Boomers/"Seniors") – Design and building of facilities – New forms of certification

Table 6 — (continued)

Topic	Key issues	Government departments/ policy areas affected
Immigration	Attracting Boomers to warmer climates/safer environments for semi-retirement or retirement will be an important new revenue-producing strategy for regions or even countries	– Immigration regulations – Tax policy – Facilities development (particularly partnerships with North American–based health providers, real estate companies, security companies) – Marketing communications
Tourism	Current focus on "packaging" established tourist favorites so as to be more accessible to "older" tourists; future focus on creating new attractions, merchandise them more flexibly; e.g., long-stay vacations combining leisure, education and other "experiences," medical tourism, spiritual and volunteer tourism and more	– Hotels and tourism – Education – Housing – Banking and infrastructure – Transportation – Marketing communications

Even the most cursory scan of these topics, and of the public policy issues they trigger, shows how significant the impact of BoomerAging will be. Quite apart from the biggie — health — BoomerAging will spill into every area of government activity, from taxation and fiscal policy to education to immigration to industrial development to science and technology. Yet today's political leaders demonstrate virtually no sign of interest.

I'm not raising this in order to complain; I'm not trying to make any kind of moral point about unfairness. BoomerAging is not an equal opportunity topic; it demands attention for the most hard-nosed reasons of practical politics: that's where the future votes will be found.

Lyndon Johnson said, famously, that the first and most important talent for a politician was to be able to count. If for no other reason that that, today's crop of political leaders are astonishingly obtuse.

Let's prove it.

Let's imagine a political party devoted exclusively to the interests of the Baby Boomers and older.

In fact, we'll use Moses Znaimer's label for this group — Zoomers.

Let's imagine a party that is so focused on this group that it literally names itself for them — the Zoomer Party.

Fatuous, you say? A silly conceit?

Watch closely.

We start by calculating the number of voters in each age group. To do this, we take the population in each age group, multiplied by the percentage that actually voted in a recent national election. For the purposes of developing this chart, I've used government statistics from each country — the US federal election of 2004, the Canadian federal election of 2004 and the British national election of 2006. Here are the numbers:

Table 7 — Voting rates and number of voters in major age groups
(population and voter figures in 'ooos)

| | CANADA | | | USA | | | UK | | |
Age	Pop	% Voted	# Voters	Pop	% Voted	# Voters	Pop	% Voted	# Voters
18–24	2,871	37	1,062	27,807	42	11,679	4,743	45	2,134
25–44	10,509	50	5,255	82,134	52	42,710	14,428	62	8,945
45–64	8,958	70	6,271	71,014	66	46,869	12,101	80	9,681
65+	4,321	70	3,025	34,376	68	23,377	8,169	87	7,107

Now we combine the 45–64 and 65+ age groups to arrive at a "Zoomer" total. And we express each age group's total number of voters as a percentage of the grand total of all voters. The results are amazingly consistent across the three countries.

Table 8 — Number and percentage of voters who are Zoomers

	CANADA		USA		UK	
	# (000)	%	# (000)	%	# (000)	%
18–24	1,062	6.8	11,679	9.4	2,134	7.7
25–44	5,255	33.7	42,710	34.3	8,945	32.1
Zoomers	9,295	59.5	70,246	56.4	16,788	60.2
Total, all groups	15,612	100.0	124,635	100.0	27,868	100.0

In all three countries, Zoomers account for about 60% of the ballots actually cast. The "youth vote" ranges from a low of 6.8% in Canada to a high of 9.4% in the USA; the 25–44 vote is close to a third. The sheer size of the Zoomer segment, multiplied by its much higher percentage turnout at the ballot box, makes Zoomers by far the dominant segment of the electorate. Here's what the gap looks like graphically:

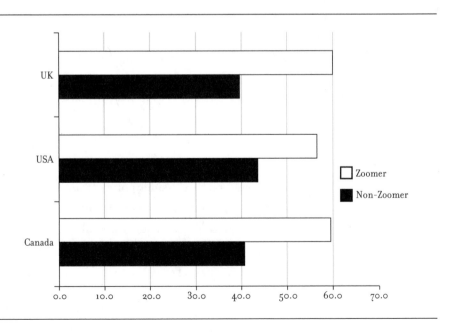

Political junkies could accuse me of forcing the issue a bit: there's no guarantee, they would argue, that all the Zoomers would vote the same way. True. But even conceding that, isn't it remarkable that all political parties seem to be ignoring a group that makes up 60% of the people who actually cast ballots?

And as for my "Zoomer Party" idea being frivolous . . .

In a survey conducted by AARP in 2004, 56% of Boomers said the USA needed a new strong third political party.

The survey found that Boomers were less loyal to the existing political parties than their parents' generation, and more likely to vote based on issues. "The message of the survey for both political parties is simple," reported *AARP* magazine. "If you think you know Boomers, think again. Portrayed as liberal during the 1960s, the majority of Boomers, now comfortably middle-aged and moving into positions of power, hold decidedly liberal positions on some issues (e.g., abortion, gun control, stem cell research) but they also endorse some conservative values. For example, they overwhelmingly support the death penalty, harsher prison sentences and school prayer." In fact, only 20% of Boomers described themselves as "very" or "moderately" liberal. And only 32% of them said they trust the government to do what is right all or most of the time.

The survey found that Boomers are less likely than their parents' generation "to believe that they owe the country certain obligations, including military service, paying taxes, and paying attention to political issues." The survey noted:

> The fact that Boomers are more open to social arrangements and behaviors that their parents would rarely consider points to an idea of politics that has less to do with regulating or prescribing behavior and more to do with allocating resources. The self-interest implied in this politics of resource allocation is evident in Boomers' approach to entitlements. Although they are more liberal on certain moral and social issues than their predecessors and expect a lot of things from government, this does not necessarily translate into support for social welfare programs or traditional entitlements. Boomers are less likely

than GIs to favor welfare programs for lower income people and far more likely to support privatizing Social Security and Medicare.

What all this means for politics and the political process we have called "tailored engagement." That is, Boomers can be expected to be as active as their parents in the political process but it will be on issues they consider important, and in ways they think are efffective. Boomers will be the last to appear at a political rally in which there is no discussion of issues that clearly affect them. They will be the last to support a candidate because of party affiliation, or only because of a general sense that he or she would make a good legislator. Tailored engagement means that political participation by Boomers will be more like the social engagement of their youth — socially active but skeptical about politics; concerned with their communities or other things that directly affect them; results oriented with more regard for producing benefits than for achieving higher goals or fulfilling moral imperatives; and conducted through arrangements that may neglect the traditional political structures to which their parents felt an allegiance.

This perfectly reflects the BoomerAging attitudes I've been describing throughout this book.

On balance, these findings ought to be slightly more encouraging for small-c conservative parties.

Now if only someone would tell them.

But then again, you and I will never figure out what goes through the minds of politicians. It's time to focus on what you *can* do something about — making sure that your particular organization, at least, is able to meet the challenges and capitalize on the opportunities of BoomerAging.

Let's get started.

PART FOUR: SO WHAT ARE YOU SUPPOSED TO DO NOW?

CHAPTER 10 **Look in the mirror**

The topic of Boomers and BoomerAging is on the edge of becoming a priority for many organizations. Within a few years, it will become *the* issue for almost everyone:

- **If you market products or services**, in most categories it will become increasingly difficult, if not impossible, to make your numbers without attracting Boomers.
- **If you run a government department, educational or social services organization**, your policies and programs will become increasingly irrelevant unless they take Boomers and BoomerAging into account.

The topic *is* starting to heat up. Although I was able to devote a whole section to the obtuseness of many organizations and institutions, it's also true that more of them *are* beginning to see what's happening, and moving to take advantage of it. This is particularly evident in the fields most directly connected to BoomerAging, such as health, money and travel.

Once this reaches the tipping point, of course, there will be a flood of corporate busy-work. Much of it will be of the panic variety, leading to a combination of ringing declarations accompanied by superficial band-aids. Acknowledging the power of Boomers and the BoomerAging process will become a necessary mark of organizational competence ("See? We get it!"). Advertising dollars will be moved around. Boomers and "seniors" will be added to brochures. There will be an avalanche of Boomer-related articles circulated around offices, with little "FYI" or "Any ideas?" sticky notes attached. (Hopefully, a zillion copies of this book will be purchased.) Most organizations, after all, know how to look committed once a trend is underway; nobody wants to be seen as being left behind.

But there's a big difference between optics and substance. Relatively few organizations, I am afraid, will have the courage to deal readily with this tidal wave of change in a meaningful way. I use the word "courage" quite deliberately. BoomerAging will require organizations to re-think every aspect of their operations, of what they offer and how they offer it.

In the next two chapters, we'll examine two critical aspects of that re-thinking process. In this chapter, we'll discuss taking a fresh look at your organization in the context of Boomers and BoomerAging. We'll deal with three topics in particular — your products or services, how you deliver them to the marketplace (your "customer experience") and how your organization operates.

In this chapter, we'll deal with some of the key issues in how you go about taking a fresh look

In the following chapter, we'll focus on communications: what your message is, who's preparing it, how it's delivered and how you can do much better.

Let me acknowledge, right off the top, that I'm not trying to replace — in just a few chapters — what would be a comprehensive review run by professionals. I have no intention in engaging in quick-and-dirty management consulting on the fly; nor am I so arrogant as to believe I could offer a few suggestions, a worksheet or two, and expect you to accept it as a serious substitute for your own thorough planning process.

My goal is simply to *provoke your thinking*.

I want to point you to areas that deserve further exploration and probing, and suggest some uncomfortable questions you ought to consider. Look at this material as an agenda, if you will, for the more substantive work you will want to undertake — you will *need* to undertake — in order to respond effectively to both the challenges and the opportunities of Boomer-Aging.

In preparing this material, I've tried to consider what *all* organizations need, regardless of the specifics of your particular industry or product/service mix:

- You could be in a business, like health or travel, selling to the most direct and immediate needs of Boomers (lucky you).
- You could be selling products or services suitable to all age groups but beginning to realize that the Boomers (and older) will soon account for the largest share of your sales.
- You could be an educational institution, or non-profit organization, looking at medium- to longer-term projections and wondering how BoomerAging will affect your model.
- You could be a government department or agency realizing that many of your policy and operational premises are about to become very dated (at best) or possibly even obsolete.

THINK 50 YEARS OUT

Notice I didn't say, "**Plan** 50 years out" or "**Act** 50 years out." Almost all of what you wind up doing will be very much in the here and now. But there should always be at least one part of your brain — and, ideally, of your organization's brain — that is thinking 50 years out and is floating questions like these:

- Where is all this going? What are the logical extensions of BoomerAging?
- What happens when people have enough life span to start an entirely new career at 50? At 60?
- What does our organization look like when our middle management are trying to understand our best customers and our best customers are 50 years older than those middle managers? How about 100 years older? How do we train front-line workers to deal with people who may be as old as their great-grandparents but who behave like their parents? And who does that training, anyway?
- What does our organization look like when some employees are a half-century older than other employees? Or a century older?

- What does our organization look like when BoomerAging swings the entire pendulum the other way, and *nobody cares about young people?* How do we recruit? Train? How do we offset the *harmful* effects of BoomerAging on organizations — i.e., a relentless "follow the money" thought process that, in the interests of making this quarter's numbers, turns it back on younger, poorer shoppers? And what is the attitude of those younger shoppers, anyway? How do they feel about growing up in a world where all the clout — and all the attention of the marketplace — is focused on people who are decades older, and orders of magnitude wealthier, than they are? Can BoomerAging become so powerful that we will need a counter-strategy someday? And if so, who develops it? A 90-year-old VP of Marketing?
- What does society look like — what do our political institutions look like — when a significant number of the same people can be . . .
  - left-wing
  - right-wing
  - taxpayers
  - tax avoiders
  - users of the system
  - bypassers of the system
  . . . all at the same time?

Some of these questions are crazy (deliberately so).

Some of these questions can't possibly be answered — or at least, not with any accuracy just yet. But it's important to ask them, because it forces a climate that recognizes BoomerAging as the revolution it really is. Otherwise, you'll spend all of your time in nickel-and-dime incrementalism — "Yes, the society is aging blah blah blah so we better get a few more old folks in the ads."

But if you think 50 years out — or at least, if you devote even 10% of your time to thinking 50 years out — you'll automatically be confronting the depth and breadth of what BoomerAging is, and what it will cause. And *that awareness alone* will act as a goad, a challenge, maybe even an inspiration, to the way you attack the more immediate issues.

So even as you rush from focus group to focus group, or brief legions of management consultants, please make sure to indulge in some "far-out" scenarios and wildly speculative questions. At minimum, it will keep the creative juices flowing. More likely, it will produce some fascinating opportunities you would never have arrived at by being only logical and linear.

A fresh look at your organization

There are many ways to go about it, and many variables depending on exactly what kind of business or service you are in. But I think it comes down to three key issues:

- **Your products or services:** what it is you are offering to the marketplace
    - How do they respond (or not respond) to Boomers and BoomerAging?
    - How could you "repackage" them?
    - What new products or services are logical extensions of what you're doing?

- **How those products or services are delivered:** your "customer experience"
    - What does a "customer" have to go through to deal with your organization?
    - Does this demonstrate responsiveness to the needs/wants/demands of Boomers, or not?
    - What could / should / must change?

- **How your organization operates:** the climate or culture that drives the decision-making
    - Are the leaders of your organization aware of or worried about this issue?
    - Do you have the talent pool to deal with it adequately?

Your products or services

Your products or services must be evaluated in the context of what Boomers want, and how they themselves evaluate what's on offer. This doesn't mean, of course, that you necessarily must respond to each and every Boomer-mandated driver of "success." You could certainly make decisions to take a pass on specific Boomer needs or wants, either because it would cost too much to meet them, or because they lie outside the scope of your "core business."

These kinds of decisions are simply the daily menu of strategic management; they take on no additional "magic" merely because they involve Boomers. (They probably do take on additional weight, though, because the Boomer market is so big.) What's important is that these decisions be made with full understanding of what the Boomer drivers actually *are* — and not by accident or default.

Here are the major drivers:

1. Health and well-being
Boomers want to live longer, and be as healthy and active as possible for as long as possible. Any product or service that can be shown to contribute to that goal will command attention.

2. Quality of life
BoomerAging means *not* having to compromise on your quality of life. BoomerAging includes a strong appeal to hedonism, to surrounding one's self with interesting and enjoyable things, and to enjoying, and benefiting from, technology.

3. A feeling of youthfulness
Boomers act 10–15 years younger than their chronological age. A product or service that "reads" as being for "old people" (even if, rationally, it *is* so) will be a turn-off. A product or service that says, "You've still got the magic" will be coveted.

4. Exploration, discovery, new adventures and experiences
BoomerAging means new experiences — maybe to the point of re-inventing one's self. A product or service that has an *experience* built into it will have a strong advantage. Anything that speaks to education, exploration, adventure, trying something new will generate strong interest.

5. Independent living

In their minds, the Boomers are going into a nursing home . . . *never*. Products or services that enhance their home environment, making it easier/safer/more comfortable/more convenient for them to live independently will command a strong and growing market.

6. Fashion, style, sex appeal

Boomers want to look good, feel good and be *seen* to be that way by others. The cosmetics industry is already on to this; the fashion (apparel) industry has been much slower but shows signs of waking up. Anything that helps Boomers look and feel *physically* the way they see themselves *mentally* will be a winner. But even if you are not directly in these product categories, if you can convey the idea that *you* have this image of your Boomer customers (for example, in the way you picture them in your communications), you'll build a strong emotional relationship that can be leveraged very positively for your business.

7. Exceptionally high levels of service

Boomers — let's face it — can be *very* high-maintenance customers. They demand exceptional service: highly personalized, anticipating their needs and delivering superior quality for the price. This is particularly critical if you're in a "me-too" product or service category — if you can design a customer experience around service, this can be a decisive point of differentiation for you.

8. Convenience

In some ways, an extension of 7. Boomers not only want a convenient shopping experience, they want products and services that are easy to use. (The flip side: they hate products or services that are difficult to use, and this again speaks to the customer experience as well as to the product itself. I will have a lot more to say about this in the discussion on "touchpoints," below).

With these drivers in mind, you can now do a quick scan of your existing product and service mix to see how it stacks up. The worksheet on page 175 makes it simple: you evaluate each product or service against each of the key drivers. The form is designed to cover only one product or service, so you'll need to make photocopies to work through your entire lineup. No need for a lot of fancy prose; just jot down a few key ideas in point form. Getting you thinking about the issues is as important as developing a "final" detailed list.

How your product or services are delivered

As important as the actual products or services are, *how they get delivered* is just as vital. In fact, I could argue that in an increasingly commoditized world, it is the *delivery* — the total customer experience associated with your product or service — that is the key differentiator. Here is where you show customers that you understand them. Or not. Here is where you build profitable relationships. Or blow them.

I like to think of delivery in terms of "touchpoints." A touchpoint is simply a point of contact between your organization and your customer or constituent. It could be a store, an office, a package, a brochure, a phone call — every venue in which a customer can interact with your organization is a touchpoint.

And for each touchpoint, it is possible to describe what kind of experience would be a positive or competitive response to the imperatives of BoomerAging, and what kind of experience would be a negative or uncompetitive response. Once the "ideal" experiences were understood, you could then analyze all of your organization's touchpoints to see how they stack up.

Touchpoint analysis is very important because it protects against, quite frankly, believing your own bullshit. It's easy to *say* the right things; easy to force-feed a couple of Boomerish photos into your environment. It's quite another to *deliver* a customer experience that shows Boomers you really understand them. For that to happen, all of the touchpoints have to be working in sync — a single disconnect can fatally undermine your credibility. And believe me, the Boomers *know* when they're being conned.

Touchpoint analysis is a well-established marketing discipline; there are a variety of approaches to it, and even some (fairly expensive) software products that could help you. Your marketing people should certainly be able to put together a touchpoint analysis. It can be a lengthy, exhaustive (and sometimes expensive) process, but done properly it is well worth the

WORKSHEET #1 — YOUR PRODUCTS AND SERVICES

Brief description of the product or service being evaluated

Key driver	How competitive is the product or service as it exists today?	How could the product or service be repositioned? Could some of its attributes be communicated more strongly, so as to appeal to this key driver?	How could the product or service be modified or improved, so as to appeal to this key driver more effectively?	What entirely new products or services could we introduce, within our overall category of business, to appeal to this key driver more effectively?
Health and well-being				
Quality of life				
Feeling of youthfulness				
Opportunity to explore, discover, etc.				
Independent living				
Fashion, style, sex appeal				
Exceptionally high levels of service				
Convenience				

effort. For the purposes of this chapter, I am simply going to review some of the major touchpoints that exist in most organizations and suggest what kind of customer experience is required in order to meet the demands of BoomerAging.

1. Storefront or first point of contact

The physical point of contact is very important because it requires a mix of obvious appeals to Boomers, and much less obvious appeals. You have to design an environment that is simultaneously exciting and dynamic — thus appealing to the emotional desires of the audience — and yet comfortable and convenient, and thus very sensitive to certain physical needs and limitations. Eyesight, for example, begins to deteriorate in one's 40s — so your signage should be easy-to-read, with large type and high-contrast color schemes. Ramps and escalators are better than stairs. Directional signing should be simple and easy to follow.

At the same time, you want to begin to communicate the benefits of your products or services — not just dry, factual descriptions of them. If you have visuals of your target customers "in action" — i.e., enjoying the products — it's imperative that you include some youthful-looking, energetic Boomers (it's astonishing how many stores make the jump from 20-something to "seniors").

2. In-store or facility — layout, design, customer experience

Inside the store or facility, you continue the same logic as with the storefront — make it physically easy while at the same time communicating emotional satisfaction. If your products or service relate directly to Boomers — particularly if they involve health or money or experiences — then bring this to life with high-energy signage and not just directional or "bare-bones" informational signage. Use active verbs wherever possible — *discover, experience, enjoy* — and plenty of photos of who you think the Boomers are. The net impression should be, "This is a place for you" rather than "Well, okay, we can cater to you if you insist." I know this sounds obvious, but it's astonishing how many stores or offices have no idea how to do this.

At all costs, avoid a separate area for "seniors." If you absolutely must — i.e., if you happen to be offering products or services only for the "older" customer — use category descriptions rather than demographic descriptions. *Pension information here*, while hardly exciting, is better than *seniors here*.

3. In-store or facility — personnel

Here's where it is easiest to go wrong . . . badly wrong.

A couple of years ago I attended a conference where a senior marketing executive of a major consumer electronics chain presented an internal video he'd produced to educate his top management on how badly their stores were catering to Boomers — particularly male Boomers shopping for big-ticket electronics.

A customer would come in — a man in his 50s, let's say — looking to buy a home theater. Nothing serious, a purchase of about $5,000 or more. He'd be greeted by a 20-something sales associate who — assuming you could pry him off the cell phone conversation he was having with his girlfriend — quickly unleashed a volley of tech-y questions, and when the customer couldn't answer, dismissed him as some lower order of species. The condescension was palpable — the sales associate saw himself as cool, savvy, up-to-the-minute; the customer was an old fart, someone who didn't even know — can you *imagine?* — the difference between LCD and plasma. The customer often walked out without making a purchase.

The top management, of course, were horrified at the picture being presented of what was going on in their stores. Tens of millions of dollars in advertising — in a ruthlessly competitive market category — to bring consumers *into* the store, only to have them driven right back out again by these patronizing kids masquerading as "sales associates." They undertook an immediate re-training program which, at last report, was still going on and hadn't been completely successful.

Condescension has two sides, of course. The other manifestation is that overly helpful "there, there, dear" approach. Again, it's usually offered by a youngish "sales associate" or "customer service representative" who assumes that everyone over the age of 50, or certainly 60, is borderline senile and utterly helpless.

The best bet, of course, is to have Boomers wait on Boomers. That way, generational misunderstandings are reduced to near zero. But if you must have staff in their 20s or 30s, make sure they are drilled on the basic of Boomers and BoomerAging. (Buy them all a copy of this book.) They must understand that the customer/client/person on the other side of the table is someone who sees himself/herself — and who therefore wants to be seen — as a person who is vital, active, ready and able to spend, but demanding. And that condescension is absolutely fatal. (In an ideal world, a firing offense.)

4. Product packaging

I would repeat many of the same points as I made for in-store signage: large type, easy-to-read; include Boomers in any shots of customers using the product; and stress end-use benefits and not just product features.

5. Product or service literature

Here again, the same points about execution — art, type, lots of active verbs in the copy. But over and above these basics, I think there are some additional opportunities to really lock in on the Boomers:

    a. Promote an online organization of users, where they can get additional product info, tips on usage, etc. — make the website identification very prominent.

    b. Ask for their feedback — give them a web address to which they can post comments about the product, about the quality of the packaging and instructional material, etc.

    c. Include a video.

    d. Include a catalogue of related products, easy to order online.

    All of these steps say to the consumer, "We value you — we know you are important and we want to hear what's on your mind; we also want to give you lots of other ways to enjoy this product (or service) and related products. Let's be important to each other!"

6. Ordering and delivery

Convenience, convenience, convenience. Customers should be able to schedule deliveries for a convenient time, and to track delivery progress over the Internet. (These are hardly radical ideas anymore.) Consider a post-delivery satisfaction check-up: a call from a live person asking if everything is okay. That live person should continue as the customer relations point of contact; the Boomer is a high-value customer who should be made to feel extremely valuable to your organization.

7. Call center and other telephone interaction

Get to a live voice as soon as possible! Do not have a recorded voice continue to say, "Your call is important to us." (The Boomer knows this is not true, and that if your phone system is so highly automated, the ugly reality is that talking to customers is the absolutely *last* thing you are interested in doing.) Once a live person does come on the line to deal with the Boomer, have as few hand-offs to other departments as possible.

8. Media advertising

I have a whole chapter on this coming up, so at this point all I will say is: the enemy is *condescension*. Also, avoid the word "senior" like the plague.

9. PR and corporate image

Understand that if items 1 through 8 are messed up, there's no saving it with clever PR or image spinning. In the first place, it's too late; in the second place, you're already playing to the most cynical and skeptical audience of all time. (These are the people who grew up on TV, remember?) To the extent that PR strategy *is* meaningful, though, I would put a premium on the word *authenticity*. If Boomers aren't your number one audience, and you're only marketing a handful of products or services for them, don't pretend otherwise. Don't make promises you can't keep; don't make ringing declarations that everyone will see as phony the moment the words are out of your mouth.

It's very important to remember that Boomers are more interested in products, services and experiences that will meet their (real or perceived) needs than in relationships with *you*. While there are a few celebrated examples that people are always quoting to show how important brands can be to Boomers (e.g., Harley-Davidson), most of the time Boomers are quite happy to jump all over the place in their shopping; they might gladly buy an individual product from a company they hate, if that particular product is compelling for them. You are absolutely *not* going to conquer them through corporate image, and I would argue that it isn't particularly necessary to try.

Oh, and one more thing, under the PR or image category:

Don't be so serious.

You may disagree with my summary of what the Boomer-sensitive attributes of the various touchpoints should be; you may want to add other specifics, based on your particular product or service category, other research you have done, etc. You can now use all those criteria to rate your own menu of touchpoints.

Worksheet #2 might be helpful. You'll see there are a couple of places in which I call for a numerical rating; in other places, you simply jot down a few comments or observations.

For the numerical rating, use a 5-point scale:

5 – SUPERIOR 4 – GOOD 3 – SATISFACTORY 2 – ONLY FAIR 1 – POOR

How your organization operates

As important as it is to take a hard look at your products or services, and how they are delivered, an even bigger factor is the culture, or operating climate, of your organization itself. The big danger here is that you will try to graft "Boomers" and "BoomerAging" onto an organization that isn't really convinced, or that has its decisions made by people who can't, or won't, get what is happening. You'll be swayed by what you see is a storm of activity all around you — "Everyone seems to be talking about Boomers and Zoomers and the aging of the population; we must get on board" — but you'll then expect solutions to be delivered by an operation that can't possibly think of them, much less execute them.

The only answer — short of replacing a lot of people — will be an aggressive program of acculturation. It doesn't matter, frankly, how strongly I urge such a program, or how credible you find my urging — events will prove how necessary it is. Organizations that adapt will thrive; organizations that don't will see continual loss of market share and profitability. The Boomers *are* where the money is . . . period. You take care of them, or you fall irretrievably behind your competitors.

WORKSHEET #2 — TOUCHPOINT RATINGS

Touchpoint	Rate on 5 → 1 scale		
	How well do we respond to Boomers and BoomerAging?	How do we compare with our competition?	What do we have to do to improve our rating?
Storefront or first point of contact			
In-store or facility — layout, design, customer experience			
In-store or facility — personnel			
Product packaging			
Product or service literature			
Ordering and delivery			
Call center and other telephone interaction			
Media advertising			
PR and corporate image			

To help you take the pulse of your organization as it now stands, I've designed a very simple questionnaire. It presents a series of statements and invites you to agree or disagree with them, using a 5-point scale:

Enter 5 if you *strongly agree* with the statement.

Enter 4 if you *somewhat agree* with the statement.

Enter 3 if you're *not sure*.

Enter 2 if you *somewhat disagree* with the statement.

Enter 1 if you *entirely disagree* with the statement.

I've deliberately framed the statements so that they don't all go in one direction — organizations that are already strongly responsive to Boomers and BoomerAging would have a mixture of both *strongly agree* and *strongly disagree* answers.

WORKSHEET #3 — YOUR PRODUCTS AND SERVICES

Indicate your agreement or disagreement with each of the statements below. Use the 5-point scale described above.

1. Boomers already represent an important market for my organization.

2. The target market specified by our media advertising buys is Adults 18–34.

3. Most of the people in our marketing department are 40 or under.

4. We have a strong training program in place to teach our field people about the needs and wants of Boomers and seniors.

5. I have had at least ten articles sent to me in the past three months from other members of my organization dealing with the aging of the population and what it means for us.

6. I have bookmarked www.50plus.com on my Internet browser because I want to see what the Boomers are reading about.

7. I subscribe to both *AARP* magazine and *CARP* magazine because I want to see what these organizations are doing.

8. In the past year, senior members of our organization have attended at least one seminar or conference dealing specifically with Boomers and aging.

9. The president of my organization has never made a comment to me about the need to go after Boomers.

10. If I gave a copy of this book to senior people in my organization, they'd think I was crazy.

11. Our HR department has a formal program in place to capture the knowledge of people who are retiring from our organization and to have them mentor younger workers.

12. We study the activities of our competitors specifically to see how they are dealing with Boomers and BoomerAging.

13. Most of my colleagues, if pushed, would probably argue that the impact of Boomers and BoomerAging is overstated.

14. Our product or service literature is always designed to take account of Boomer needs and wants.

15. I think it would be too difficult, and take too much time and expense, to cash in effectively on the trends outlined here. And besides, it's all too speculative and too far into the future.

16. We have existing programs going on in our organization right now to research and plan how we can better serve the Boomers and seniors markets.

17. Our marketing plans focus on creating brand loyalty among younger consumers; we believe the Boomers' brand loyalties are already set.

How did you do?

I deliberately didn't create a set of "right" answers or an "ideal" final score. You can make your own judgment as to where your organization falls, by comparing the statements with where you fall on the agree/disagree spectrum.

Pay particular attention to how did you do on the questions that dealt with your colleagues and their attitudes. If you become a strong advocate for this topic, will you be pushing rope — or playing into a climate of opinion that is already coalescing, in a favorable way, around this issue?

As the topic heats up, there will be a dramatic growth in the number of resources you can use: research studies, statistical reports, case histories, seminars and workshops. To keep current, you may want to consider being part of a reader network I'm putting together. I'll be emailing members of the group on a regular basis with suggestions for further reading and invitations to workshops, seminars (and online webinars) and other special events. No cost or obligation, of course. Just send me an e-mail with your coordinates, and I'll add you to the group. E-mail me at d.cravit@zoomermedia.ca and you're in.

Turning around your entire operation is a huge topic — far outside the scope of one chapter. As I noted at the beginning of this chapter, all I'm really trying to do is provoke some thinking, suggest what the key topics ought to be, indicate some of the corners you should probe into.

But there's one area where I can get a lot more specific — an area where you're probably already spending a serious sum of money: marketing communications. What about that ad budget, anyway? Is it on target? Is it effective? How can you tell? What should you do to make it work better? These are the important questions we'll now turn to.

CHAPTER 11 **Shoot the messenger**

"Half my advertising budget is wasted," complained department store magnate John Wanamaker. "The trouble is, I don't know which half."

That was over a century ago.

Since then, there have been many other notable observations about advertising. Marshall McLuhan called advertising "the greatest art form of the twentieth century" but Fairfax Cone, co-founder of the giant Foote Cone & Belding agency that is a major player to this day, was much more prosaic: "Advertising is what you do when you can't go see somebody. That's all it is."

There has been a lot of huffing and puffing about the morality of advertising. F. Scott Fitzgerald, no doubt jaded by his disastrous experience as a Hollywood screenwriter, called it "a racket, like the movies and the brokerage business." He went on to say, in a letter to his daughter, "You cannot be honest without admitting that its constructive contribution to humanity is exactly minus zero." Wife Zelda was equally critical: "We grew up founding our dreams on the infinite promise of American advertising. I still believe that one can learn to play the piano by mail and that mud will give you a perfect complexion."

People in the business are even more unsparing. Al Ries, who pioneered the concept of "positioning," said, "Today communication itself is the problem. We have become the world's first overcommunicated society. Each year we send more and receive less." And copywriter Isabelle Kuprin, explaining her job to Studs Terkel, said, "It involves being a total asshole. I do it for the money, it's easy and horrible. I do nothing good for society." The morality of taking that money from the client while sneering at the task at hand does not seem to have occurred to her.

Whatever their specific slant on the business, all critics agree that advertising exerts a huge impact on our society. Even today, when the traditional ad agency role is under attack, when the concept of "mass media" is obsolete and new models are emerging, it remains true that for most organizations media advertising represents the fastest and most convenient way to solve a host of other ills. The blunt truth is that, for all the deep analysis that I've proposed in the preceding chapter, a huge number of organizations will respond to BoomerAging *first* through their media advertising budgets. They'll take the shortcut — if they can find a way to *communicate* their products and services in relation to Boomers and BoomerAging, this will be a lot quicker and cheaper than just about any other steps they can take.

And the thing is, they're not necessarily wrong. Band-aids are certainly not a long term — or even medium-term — solution. But they're better than letting the blood continue to flow.

So I'm presenting a chapter on communications not because I think communication alone is "the answer" (and I hope the preceding chapter makes that clear), but because I think we have to be realistic here. The right kind of communication *can* put you into the game, at the very least, and provoke attention and trial while you (hopefully) work hard to adjust all the other stuff. The wrong kind of communication can simply hand the prize to your competitors.

In an earlier chapter, I walked you through the often-dysfunctional advertising and media landscape of today, with so many companies still not getting it. In this chapter, we're going to focus on what you can do — and what you should avoid like the plague.

I've broken it down to Ten Commandments:

1. Think product and product benefits — *not* demographics or psychographics.
2. Cast the product benefits in the light of *experiences*. Be daring. Show how life can be exciting, adventurous, even unconventional.
3. Do not allow anyone under the age of 40 to write copy. If you have to violate this rule, insist that any work submitted to you be read, and signed, by a parent of the copywriter.

4. Further to 3, be on the lookout for any signs of condescension or patronization in your message. Make it a firing offence to produce work that has those elements in it.

5. Do not send Boomers to your corporate website. Have a separate website that is specifically designed for them.

6. Further to 5, create as many opportunities as possible for Boomers to engage in dialogue with you and with other Boomers who use your products or services.

7. Do not use celebrities from the past unless they relate specifically to the products or services on offer. Then think big.

8. In addition to your current campaign, deliberately create campaigns that you won't be able to run until ten years from now. This will keep you constantly thinking, "Where does all this lead?" and will help you get there before your competitor.

9. Until the TV industry wakes up, your best media are the Internet, magazines and radio.

10. Remember that this audience has spent their entire lives perfecting the art of ignoring everything you have to say. Their BS meter is tremendously well calibrated.

There are other topics I considered, but rejected — particularly those that relate to Grand Strategy. It's too hard to set out a simplistic rule or two that would cover the wide range of organizations for whom Boomers and Boomer-Aging are critical; you know your own business better than I do. I think it's more helpful to cut right to the chase — the practical dos and don'ts that can make all the difference.

So let's get started.

1. Think product and product benefits — not demographics or psychographics.

This may seem counter-intuitive — hasn't this entire book been about demographics? About digging deep to understand the mind of the Boomer, the attitudes that drive Boomer behavior? Now that the decisive moment is at hand, and the time has come to start churning out ads, am I saying to forget all that and just concentrate on listing the product features?

Well, yes — in a way that's exactly what I am saying. (Except for the boring idea of "listing" — but we'll get to that in a minute.)

The trick here is to not *overthink* the demographics or psychographics. Be aware of them, yes — but don't focus on them so as to crowd out what the Boomers are really after, which is nothing more or less than interesting, relevant information that can help them live better. Overthinking the attitudinal component means you start shading the message with so much executional subtext that you lose the substance. Every Boomer (in North America, at least) can remember the classic Wendy's burgers campaign, "Where's the beef?" Take that as your mantra — substance, substance, substance. Burying the essential product information under a Grateful Dead soundtrack because you think that the music will send some kind of magic signal to the Boomers is a fatal mistake.

Besides, it shows a fundamental disrespect both for your product or service and for your audience. It says you're more worried about psyching them out than giving them important information. What does that make you? What does it make your product or service? What does it say about your attitude to the Boomers? A strong advocate of making sure you nail the product story first and foremost is Chuck Nyren, whose book, *Advertising to Baby Boomers*, is a must-read. (Check him out at http://advertisingtobaby-boomers.blogspot.com). He notes, "People don't walk around thinking about how old they are. I don't leave the house being fifty-four. Nor do I walk about feeling my age. . . . Sometimes I feel eighteen, other times eighty-six. Rarely do I feel my age, whatever that feels like. I don't know. I'm not sure I want to feel my age. I like the variety."

2. Cast the product benefits in the light of experiences. Be daring.
Show how life can be exciting, adventurous, even unconventional.
This is, to some extent, just me being an old-time ex–ad agency practitioner who is indulging in a bit of a curmudgeonly moment. The fact is, far too much of today's advertising worships creativity for its own sake and fails to communicate the benefits of actually *buying* and *using* whatever it is you're selling. Let me stay on this soapbox for at least a paragraph or so. All ad agencies, to at least some degree, are award chasers — and this particularly applies to their young creative staffs who seem more interested in their

résumés than in actually, ahem, moving carloads of the client's products. In many award-winning campaigns, it is difficult to discern exactly what is being sold, let alone what its benefits are.

Okay. Rant finished; I got it off my chest. Your agency may or may not be guilty of these sins, but when it comes to the Boomer audience I can assure you that these tendencies really *are* sins. It's not that your creative product should be boring; it's not that the Boomers will automatically reject anything clever or edgy. But it's much more important to communicate clearly and to *demonstrate* the benefits of the product or service.

Besides, I can think of nothing more creatively exciting than to show your products or services *in the context of BoomerAging*. Here is a real revolution, a generation that is shattering all the traditional ideas of what it means to age. And your product or service is playing a role in that new kind of experience. Showing that role — bringing that experience to life — ought to be a creative assignment people would kill for.

One important caveat: demonstrate, don't preach. Don't talk *at* them — don't tell them why they need your product or service, simply show it in action. Show other Boomers using it, benefiting from it — let the audience draw its own conclusions. The moment you become too declarative, up goes the BS screen — and believe me, this is a generation that has spent a lifetime perfecting that screen (see point 10).

3. **Do not allow anyone under the age of 40 to write copy. If you have to violate this rule, insist that any work submitted to you be read, and signed, by a parent of the copywriter.**

I am completely serious. You are playing for tens of millions of dollars (perhaps much more) — how can you let the message be created by people who are 20 or 30 years younger than the target audience? Especially since these people, in the experience of most observers of the ad scene (including, very emphatically, yours truly), have demonstrated not even the slightest ability to understand and communicate with Boomers?

If it were up to me, I would insist that your ad agency immediately replace the entire creative team with Boomers. Nobody understands this market better than the people who are in it.

If that's impossible, require your copywriters to get a signed note from one of their parents before they submit any work to you. That note should say that the proposed ad, commercial or whatever has been read by the parent and that the parent did not either roll his/her eyes or burst into hysterical laughter or want to punch the writer.

4. **Further to 3, be on the lookout for any signs of condescension or patronization in your message. Make it a firing offence to produce work that has those elements in it.**

The severity of item 3 is necessary because of the thus-far-constant tendency of messages aimed at Boomers to be patronizing or condescending. It's as if the advertisers can't quite bring themselves to believe that the audience is capable of understanding, much less dealing with, the "modern" content of the product or service — particularly if it involves technology. This condescension manifests itself in a number of ways:

- Overly specific references to age, juxtaposed with references to how one is "supposed to" feel or react — e.g., "When you get to this age, you need . . ." or "When you get to this age, you want . . . "
- Depictions of Boomers and "seniors" as being helpless, confused, incapable.
- Depictions of Boomers and "seniors" as being passive, at the end of the line, quietly playing out the script to a (hopefully) gentle finish.
- Expressions of surprise or delight, on the part of younger onlookers, whenever a Boomer or "senior" manages something — again, this particularly applies to technology. Kids who can't quite believe that mom or dad are able to log on to the Internet or manage an iPod, for example.

5. **Do not send Boomers to your corporate website. Have a separate website that is specifically designed for them.**

I think this is a valid tactic for any age group, not just Boomers. It's too fast, inexpensive and flexible to create a microsite for you to be wasting time driving everything to a one-size-fits-all corporate website.

So what would be the differences between a Boomer-targeted site and an all-purpose "corporate" destination?

- Slightly larger font size — but not too large, as if you were trying to make a point on a point.
- More intuitive navigation — A therefore B, B therefore C.
- More information and less creative "flash-for-its-own-sake."
- Online ordering of every conceivable thing you can think of — Boomers want to shop online because it's fast and convenient and eliminates extra steps (like a visit to your store) that they're not all that excited about in the first place.
- Interactivity that enhances the flow of information.
- Highly personalized blogs, videos, etc. by people associated with the product or service — personalize your organization and open up genuine dialogue; it's an easy way to say "service" to a high-maintenance generation.

6. **Further to 5, create as many opportunities as possible for Boomers to engage in dialogue with you and with other Boomers who use your products or services.**

This is really an expansion of the two points above, but they do warrant some extra commentary.

In one sense, it's dangerous to generalize about Boomers, because there is no one set of attitudes and behaviors that fits them all. That said, I think it's fair to claim that, taken as a whole, they are very interested in high levels of service, and in being treated as important customers. After all, they've been that way all their lives — and it's only now, as they butt up against the traditional frontiers of "oldness," that they discover marketers are no longer all that interested in them. That indifference is changing, of course, and you can be sure that the organizations that deliver high levels of service and individual attention will reap tremendous benefits, both in terms of higher sales and market share, and in terms of materially weakening their competitors.

Remember, too, that Boomers have spent their lifetimes being cynical about advertising and suspicious of the claims of marketers, particularly where those claims have to do with the marketers' stated attitudes toward the customers. "Your call is important to us" — a staple of the automated telephone responses that are the norm in business today — is perhaps the most exquisite expression of "We couldn't care less about you, or why else would we substitute this recorded message for a real live person?" Eventually, all these pious expressions of corporate goodwill — so blatantly unfulfilled in the customer's real-life experience — become just background noise, and all large organizations morph into the same remote, indifferent, incompetent blob, to be navigated around rather than engaged.

Which leaves a pretty big vacuum for someone to do it right. Why not you?

The Internet provides a very quick way of achieving this. A Boomer-focused site can provide many opportunities to solicit feedback, create dialogue (between Boomers and your organization, as well as between Boomers and each other), and give your organization a human face. Consider:

- Polls, surveys and other feedback devices
- The opportunity to rate products and services
- Chat and forums, where your site can become a meeting place for Boomers to exchange news, ideas, comments, etc.
- Podcasts, webinars and other online events, both in real time and archived
- Virtual trade shows, fairs, exhibits, conventions
- Blogs and videos from your corporate executives, with talkback features for the audience
- Value-added "clubs" that offer enhanced services (or discounts) to frequent shoppers

The technology to execute every one of these things already exists, and Boomers (surprise, surprise) are already heavy users. Remember, they are actively seeking relevant and helpful information.

7. **Do not use celebrities from the past unless they relate specifically to the products or services on offer. Then think big.**
One of the sure signs that some marketers are finally waking up to Boomers and BoomerAging is the number of new ad campaigns that feature the icons,

and the music, that Boomers grew up with. In an earlier chapter, we talked about Diane Keaton and Susan Sarandon promoting cosmetics (L'Oréal Paris and Revlon, respectively), but there's a lot more. Sir Paul McCartney has pitched Fidelity financial planning, and Dennis Hopper is the focus of a financial planning campaign by Ameriprise. Cadillac ran — and then dropped — a campaign featuring the music of Led Zeppelin. Other advertisers have used songs like "Daydream" by the Lovin' Spoonful (1966), "On the Road Again" by Canned Heat (1968) and "Gimme Some Lovin'" by the Spencer Davis Group (1967).

In fact, as reported in an article by Stuart Elliott in the *New York Times* in September, 2007, there's a bit of a trend to evoke the 1960s in order to pitch products to Boomers. Brands like Geico insurance, Lucky jeans, Total cereal and US Trust have all hopped on board the bandwagon. "What is most intriguing about the trend," writes Elliott, "is that the ads present many of the contentious aspects of the '60s — the protests, the hippies, the challenge to authority — in a positive, even romanticized light. For instance, a trippy-looking commercial for Total, sold by General Mills, begins, 'The '60s were about change, defying convention,' and ends by proclaiming the cereal as the best breakfast 'for mind and body.'"

Predictably, the advertisers all claim the campaigns are working. For example, the article quotes Ann Hayden, worldwide creative director on the General Mills (Total cereal) account at ad agency Saatchi & Saatchi in New York: "A lot of people are noticing . . . it gives us a starting point for getting people to re-think the brand."

Well, okay.

If she says so. (And, to be fair, Total has a great website that incorporates a lot of the ideas I have proposed in point 6 — check it out at www.totalcereal.com.)

But I would urge caution.

It's not that the idea of using Boomer celebrities or music is inherently bad. It's that it can quickly become bad if it's seen as a substitute for relevant information about the product or service.

Chuck Nyren is scathing in his view of this tactic when applied as indiscriminately as it now seems to be. Here's a comment from his blog:

Purely anecdotal: I'm watching TV. I hear a tune I haven't heard in thirty-five, forty years. My mind goes off into the ether. "Wow. What a great song. I'd forgotten all about it. I had the album. The cover was blue . . . And there were a bunch of other great songs on that album. What the hell were they? I can't remember . . . I wonder if I can get it on Amazon. There's probably only a compilation of his hits, or a boxed set. But I just want the CD of the album. I'll have to remember to check the next time I'm online . . ." By then, the commercial is over. In fact, probably three other commercials are over. I have no idea what the product is, or what any of the other products are.

That's one trap, of course. They remember the face or the tune, and because it is a purely executional gimmick having no relationship to the product or service, they completely tune out whatever it is you're selling.

Worse, the whole effort can come off as manipulative and insincere. It's as if you're telegraphing the fact that your 20-something copywriter — being clueless about this audience — did some research and dug up a few celebrities or hit tunes and sold you on it as a quick and dirty way to say, "You see? We get it. We understand you. Look — here's Donovan, here's a painted Volkswagen Beetle, here's a peace sign . . . " And that's supposed to make everything okay.

What you may really be saying to the audience, however, is more like this: "We don't understand you at all. We can't figure out why our product or service is meaningful to you, and if it is, we certainly don't know how to explain it. So instead, we're gluing this piece of nostalgia on to our message, even though it really has nothing to do with what we sell."

How do you distinguish between what's real and what's BS?

When they pitch you the idea, make them explain — *specifically* — why the icon, the music, the symbol, whatever, is *relevant* to the message. "That's what the Boomers know, that's they grew up with" is not — I repeat, *not* — a satisfactory answer. If it was, Virgin Mobile would be using Mr. Snuffle-upagus to market cell phones to teenagers.

8. **In addition to your current campaign, deliberately create campaigns that you won't be able to run until ten years from now. This will keep you constantly thinking, "Where does all this lead?" and will help you get there before your competitor.**

In a previous chapter, I urged you to devote at least a small portion of your brain to thinking 50 years out. Here's the ad version of that advice: where does all this go ten years from now? The youngest Boomers will be 54, the majority will be over 60, and the oldest will be just over 70. What then? What does the message say? What does the ad look like? What's happening on the website?

You don't have to jump abruptly to a whole new world. Just lay out the logical extensions of what you're doing — or about to be doing — right now. Above all, think about the team that has to get you there. Do you have the right players?

9. **Until the TV industry wakes up, your best media are the Internet, magazines and radio.**

This is not intended to be a treatise on media buying. The range of options, costs, efficiencies and success factors vary too much, depending on what type of organization you are, what your strategy is and where you're located. So I can make only some general observations — things to think about as you deal with your ad agency or media buying service:

- Boomers grew up with TV and love TV, but as we have seen the TV industry seems to be doing everything it can to drive them away. Until that changes, other media will get you there more quickly and efficiently. (And besides, the Internet is likely to become TV in any case.)
- Boomers like to read, and are hungry for information. The Internet is the fastest and most convenient medium for product research, and magazines offer the most-focused and in-depth coverage of specific topics.
- Radio also offers efficient reach. The audiences are growing older as the kids abandon the radio stations in favor of their iPod.

10. **Remember that this audience has spent their entire lives perfecting the art of ignoring everything you have to say. Their BS meter is tremendously well calibrated.**

The Boomers were the first generation to have no memory of life without TV. They grew up with it as the dominant medium. Among other things, this has made them very skeptical and cynical about advertising. They are not brand loyal, contrary to the received wisdom of the marketing/advertising industry, and they prefer information to hype. Do not assume that they are easy to sell. In particular, be wary of creative gimmickry in place of meaningful information.

On the plus side, if you do have good information, you will find an audience that is not only receptive to it but actively seeking it out. In fact, they are gradually taking control away from *you*. It's easy, now, to consult with their peers, to find out about other people's experiences with your product or service. The Internet enables a flow of information that is both instant and comprehensive, against which your slogan or your jingle are woefully inadequate defenses. Far better to become part of the process rather than to seek to control it:

- Be *genuine* in seeking to engage Boomers — talk to them online, in focus groups, in your storefront or other points of delivery; be curious, and be ready to learn.
- See your products or service through their eyes and in relation to the phenomena of BoomerAging that we've looked at in this book. What have you really got to offer? How does it speak to what they're after? How does it help them break the mold?
- Start with the product and the information. Forget about execution for a moment — *what is the actual story?* What are the key facts, the important product or service attributes, and how and why are these relevant? Unless and until you've pinned this down, it doesn't matter how you execute the message. Remember that this is an audience for whom creative gimmickry — technique as opposed to substance — is particularly ineffective, if for no other reason than that they have had decades of immunizing themselves from all your creativity-for-its-own-sake.

- Once you have nailed the story, make sure it's communicated clearly and that benefits are demonstrated and not just talked about. By all means dress it up with intriguing and intrusive creative devices (and this could include celebrities or Boomer music and symbols), but only to make it stand out from the crowd and to add impact, and as long as the story itself is not obscured.
- Then let the Boomers have at it. Encourage their feedback, and be the place where they can exchange views and even critical comments (they will, anyway, whether you like it or not, so you might as well be the forum) and — if you're fortunate — become advocates for your organization, and your products or services.

The good news is that they want to hear what you have to say. They're rooting for you to have solutions they can use. What they don't want — and what they'll punish, ruthlessly, in the marketplace — is fakery. They've spent too much time, and become too accomplished, at tuning out corporate phoniness. Good luck!

Stay tuned

The BoomerAging Revolution is well underway — but at the same time, it's only just beginning.

The reason I say that is that we still look at Boomer attitudes and behaviors *in relation to* "traditional" concepts of aging and of old age. Throughout this book, for example, I have talked about "oldness" — of mind, emotion, attitude and body — and contrasted it with BoomerAging. The Boomers act younger than their chronological age, I've pointed out. "Old" doesn't mean the same thing as it used to. Thus, The New Old.

But in future, these comparisons will be unnecessary — except, perhaps, in a book of history. BoomerAging will have created new norms, new definitions of what happens at every age and what is expected at every age. The generations that come in behind the Boomers will *not* be acting "younger than their chronological age" — they'll be acting in accordance with what's expected at that age, *as pioneered today by the Boomers.* What seems remarkably new and different today — the search for a 150-year-old life span (or even longer); a refusal to ever "retire"; a lifetime of employment, education or other adventures; seven decades or more of sexual activity — will simply be the way things are. But we can count on there being future revolutions to push the horizons out even further.

In the immediate future, of course, we still have to wrestle with many of the social, economic and political implications of BoomerAging. Smart organizations — even if they don't directly market to Boomers today — will want to keep an active eye on these developments. There could be some interesting (and troublesome) clashes of generations, with the shoe suddenly on the other foot as the market chases the money and rejects the youth.

One thing is for sure — this book will need frequent updating. So stay tuned. I'm only 63 — I could be writing about this topic for another 30 years or so.

If not longer.